Delish
family slow cooker

HEARST BOOKS
New York

Contents

Take It Slowly

Getting the best from your slow cooker

There's something wonderful about the aroma, flavor, and texture of a slow-cooked meal. Slow cookers are perfect for this method of cooking. First, read the manufacturer's instruction manual carefully, it will advise you to *not* leave the appliance on and unattended at any time; this, of course, is a safety measure.

These appliances are available in various shapes and sizes, and with a variety of different features. For example, some have timers that shut off after the cooking time has expired, some don't; some have timers that reduce the temperature and keep the food warm until you decide to eat. If you're in the market for a slow cooker, research the subject well: check out the cookers and their features carefully to make sure the appliance suits your needs. They are all "safe" in terms of making sure the food reaches the correct temperatures to destroy any harmful bacteria during the long slow cooking times.

We chose to test the recipes in this cookbook using a 4½-quart slow cooker, the most popular size. If you have a smaller or larger slow cooker than the one we used, you will need to decrease or increase the quantity of food, and almost certainly the liquid content, in the recipes.

Handy hints

Most recipes using red meat recommend that the meat is browned first, as if you were making a casserole. Do this in a heated, oiled, large frying pan, adding the meat in batches, and turning the meat so it browns all over. Overcrowding the pan will result in stewed,

not browned, meat. If you're pressed for time, the meat and/or vegetables can be browned the night before. Once everything is browned, put it into a sealable container, along with any juices, and refrigerate until the next day.

Some recipes suggest tossing the meat in flour before browning, some don't. Usually when the meat is floured, the finished sauce will be thick enough to make a light-coating gravy. If the meat is not floured, it might be necessary to thicken the sauce. Usually all-purpose flour or corn starch are used for thickening; corn starch results in a less cloudy sauce than if flour is used. The flour or corn starch needs to be blended with butter or a cold liquid such as water or some of the cooled sauce from the slow cooker. Stir the flour mixture into the sauce at the end of the cooking time, while the slow cooker is on the highest setting, then put the lid back on and leave the sauce to thicken— this will take 10 to 20 minutes.

As a general rule for casserole, stew, curry, and tagine recipes, the container of the slow cooker should be at least half-full. Place the vegetables into the cooker, put the meat on top of the vegetables, then add the liquid. Soups are easy, just make sure the cooker is at least half-full. Roasts, using whole pieces of meat or poultry, and pot roasts are sometimes cooked with hardly any liquid—especially if the meat is cooking on a bed of vegetables—sometimes a little liquid is added simply to make a sauce or gravy. Corned meats are usually cooked in enough liquid to barely cover them.

Some meats produce a lot of fat if cooked over a long period of time. There are a couple of gadgets available in kitchen/ cookware shops for removing fat: one is a type of "brush" that sweeps away the fat; the other is a type of cup that separates the fat from the liquid. However, one of the easiest ways to remove fat is to soak it up using sheets of absorbent paper towel on the surface. The best way of all is to refrigerate the food, the fat will set on top of the liquid, then it can simply be lifted off and discarded.

Freezing leftovers

Each recipe notes whether you can freeze it. The slow cooker's capacity allows you to cook a lot of food at once, so if there's any left over, it's smart to freeze some for another time. There is always a lot of liquid to contend with in the slow cooker, so remove the meat and vegetables to appropriate-sized freezer-friendly containers, pour in enough of the liquid to barely cover the meat, etc., seal the container, and freeze—while it's hot is fine—for up to three months. Any leftover liquid can be frozen separately and used as a base for another recipe, such as soup or a sauce.

What setting do I use?

Use the low setting for a long, all-day cooking time, or reduce the cooking time by about half if using the high setting. The food will reach simmering point on either setting. If your slow cooker has a warm setting, this is not used for actual cooking; it's used after the cooking time to maintain the food's temperature until you're ready to eat.

If you need to add ingredients or thicken the sauce after the cooking time, turn the covered slow cooker to high to get maximum heat. Remove the lid and add the ingredients or thickening, replace the lid and leave the cooker to heat the added ingredients or to thicken the sauce; this will take between 10 and 20 minutes.

Can I use any of my favorite recipes in a slow cooker?

Most soup, stew, casserole, tagine, and curry recipes are perfect to use in the slow cooker. The trick is to make sure there is enough liquid in the cooker for the long, slow, cooking time. Once you get to know the cooker, you'll be able to adapt a lot of your favorite recipes. Some roasts work well in the slow cooker, too. Use recipes that you would normally slow cook, well-covered in an oven set at a low temperature.

Also, some conventionally slow-cooked desserts and steamed pudding recipes can be prepared in the slow cooker.

What cuts of meat should I use?

Use secondary, cheaper, tougher cuts of red meat. The long, slow, cooking time will tenderize the cuts, and the flavors will be excellent; it's simply a waste to use more expensive primary cuts for this method of cooking. Other types of meat (secondary/stewing cuts) such as venison, goat, rabbit, hare, pork, etc., are suitable to use in the slow cooker.

All kinds of poultry will cook well in a slow cooker; but be careful not to overcook it because it will become stringy. If you can access mature birds, such as boiling fowls or wild duck, etc., the long, slow cooking times will tenderize the flesh, making it very flavorful.

Seafood is generally not suitable to use in a slow cooker because it toughens quickly. However, there are many recipes for sauces that marry well with seafood, and these can be cooked in the slow cooker, and the seafood added just before you're ready to serve. Large octopus will cook and become tender in a slow cooker.

Important safety tips

Read the instruction manual of the appliance carefully.

Make sure the cooker is sitting flat on the counter safely away from water, any heat source, such as gas flames, stove tops, and ovens, curtains, walls, children, and pets.

Make sure the electrical cord is away from any water or heat source, and make sure the cord is not dangling on the floor because someone may trip on it.

Make sure that no one touches any metal part of the cooker while it's in use; the metal parts do get very hot.

General cleaning

Most slow cooker inserts can be washed in hot soapy water. To remove cooked-on food, soak in warm water, then scrub lightly with a plastic or nylon brush. Never put a hot insert under cold water because this can cause the insert to break. The outer metal container should never be placed in water; just wipe the outside with a damp cloth and dry. Don't use abrasives or chemicals to clean the cooker because these can damage the surfaces.

A note on dried beans

We have used canned beans in this cookbook, but if you want to use dried beans instead, there are few things you must do to prevent food poisoning.

All kidney-shaped beans of all colors and sizes are related to each other, and must be washed, drained, then boiled in fresh water until they're tender—there's no need for overnight soaking; the time depends on the type of bean. Then, like canned beans, they can be added to the food in the slow cooker.

Soy beans and chickpeas are fine to use raw in the slow cooker, just rinse them well first; there's no need for overnight soaking before cooking them in the slow cooker.

Soups

lamb shank, fennel, and vegetable soup

serves 6

1 tablespoon olive oil
4 French-trimmed lamb shanks (2 pounds)
1 medium brown onion, chopped coarsely
2 baby fennel bulbs, sliced thinly
2 medium carrots, chopped coarsely
4 cloves garlic, crushed
2 fresh small red Thai chilies,
   chopped finely
2 teaspoons ground cumin
2 teaspoons ground coriander
1 teaspoon ground cinnamon
1 teaspoon caraway seeds
pinch saffron threads
1½ quarts water
2 cups beef stock
14½-ounce can diced tomatoes
15-ounce can chickpeas,
   rinsed, drained
¾ cup frozen baby peas
1 cup loosely packed fresh coriander
   (cilantro) leaves

1 Heat half the oil in large frying pan; cook lamb, until browned all over, then place in 4½-quart slow cooker.
2 Heat remaining oil in same pan; cook onion, fennel, carrot, garlic, and chili, stirring, until onion softens. Add spices; cook, stirring, until fragrant. Place vegetable mixture into cooker. Stir in the water, stock, undrained tomatoes, and chickpeas. Cook, covered, on low, 10 hours.
3 Remove lamb from cooker. When cool enough to handle, remove meat from bones, shred meat; discard bones. Stir meat, peas, and coriander leaves into cooker. Season to taste.

prep + cook time 10 hours 30 minutes
nutritional count per serving
6.1g total fat (1.4g saturated fat); 228 cal;
13.6g carbohydrate; 26.3g protein; 6.7g fiber

❄ suitable to freeze at the end of step 2.

serving suggestion Serve soup with lemon wedges, Greek-style yogurt, and crusty bread.

italian chicken soup

serves 6

3-pound chicken
3 large tomatoes
1 medium brown onion, chopped coarsely
2 stalks celery, trimmed, chopped coarsely
1 large carrot, chopped coarsely
2 dried bay leaves
4 cloves garlic, peeled, halved
6 black peppercorns
8 cups water
¾ cup orzo pasta
½ cup coarsely chopped fresh flat-leaf parsley
½ cup coarsely chopped fresh basil
2 tablespoons finely chopped fresh oregano
¼ cup fresh lemon juice

1 Discard as much skin as possible from chicken. Chop 1 tomato coarsely. Chop remaining tomatoes finely; refrigerate, covered, until needed.

2 Place chicken, coarsely chopped tomato, onion, celery, carrot, bay leaves, garlic, peppercorns, and the water in 4½-quart slow cooker. Cook, covered, on low, 8 hours.

3 Carefully remove chicken from cooker. Strain broth through fine sieve into large heatproof bowl; discard solids. Skim and discard any fat from broth. Return broth to cooker; add orzo and finely chopped tomatoes. Cook, covered, on high, about 30 minutes or until orzo is tender.

4 Meanwhile, when cool enough to handle, remove meat from bones; shred coarsely. Discard bones. Add chicken, herbs, and juice to soup; cook, covered, on high, 5 minutes. Season to taste.

prep + cook time 9 hours
nutritional count per serving
14.1g total fat (4.4g saturated fat); 378 cal; 23.2g carbohydrate; 37g protein; 4.5g fiber

❄ suitable to freeze at the end of step 2.

borscht

4 tablespoons butter
2 medium brown onions, chopped finely
1-pound beef chuck steak, cut into
   large chunks
1 cup water
1½ pounds beets, peeled, chopped finely
2 medium potatoes, chopped finely
2 medium carrots, chopped finely
4 small tomatoes, chopped finely
1 quart beef stock
⅓ cup red wine vinegar
3 dried bay leaves
4 cups finely shredded cabbage
2 tablespoons coarsely chopped fresh
   flat-leaf parsley
½ cup sour cream

1 Melt half the butter in large frying pan; cook onion, stirring, until soft. Place onion in 4½-quart slow cooker. Melt remaining butter in same pan; cook beef, stirring, until browned all over. Place beef in cooker. Add the water to the same pan; bring to a boil, then add beets, potatoes, carrots, tomatoes, stock, vinegar, and bay leaves to slow cooker. Cook, covered, on low, 8 hours.
2 Discard bay leaves. Remove beef from soup; shred using two forks. Return beef to soup with cabbage; cook, covered, on high, about 20 minutes or until cabbage is wilted. Stir in parsley.
3 Serve soup topped with sour cream.

prep + cook time 8 hours 50 minutes
nutritional count per serving
20.6g total fat (12.4g saturated fat); 404 cal; 25.3g carbohydrate; 25.3g protein; 8.8g fiber

❄ suitable to freeze at the end of step 1.

cream of celeriac soup

serves 6

4 pounds celeriac (celery root), peeled,
  chopped coarsely
1 medium brown onion, chopped coarsely
3 cloves garlic, quartered
1 stalk celery, trimmed, chopped coarsely
6 cups water
1 quart chicken stock
½ cup light cream
⅓ cup loosely packed fresh chervil leaves
1 tablespoon olive oil

1   Combine celeriac, onion, garlic, celery,
the water, and stock in 4½-quart slow
cooker. Cook, covered, on low, 8 hours.
2   Stand soup 10 minutes, then blend or
process, in batches, until smooth. Return
soup to cooker; stir in cream. Cook,
covered, on high, until hot; season to taste.

3   Serve soup sprinkled with chervil;
drizzle with oil.

prep + cook time 8 hours 30 minutes
nutritional count per serving
13.3g total fat (6.7g saturated fat); 238 cal;
16.8g carbohydrate; 7.1g protein; 12.6g fiber

tip   Be careful when blending or processing
hot soup—don't overfill the container (one
third to half-full as a guide), and make sure
the lid is secure.

❄ suitable to freeze at the end of step 1.

spicy red lentil and chickpea soup serves 6

2 teaspoons vegetable oil
1 medium brown onion, chopped finely
2 cloves garlic, crushed
1-inch piece fresh ginger, grated
2 teaspoons smoked paprika
1 teaspoon ground cumin
½ teaspoon dried chili flakes
12 ounces pumpkin, chopped coarsely
1 stalk celery, trimmed, sliced thickly
¾ cup red lentils
15-ounce canned chickpeas,
  rinsed, drained
14½-ounce can diced tomatoes
3 cups water
3 cups vegetable stock
⅓ cup finely chopped fresh
  flat-leaf parsley

1 Heat oil in small frying pan; cook onion, garlic, and ginger, stirring, until onion softens. Add spices and chili; cook, stirring, until fragrant.
2 Place onion mixture into 4½-quart slow cooker; stir in pumpkin, celery, lentils, chickpeas, undrained tomatoes, the water, and stock. Cook, covered, on low, 6 hours. Season to taste.
3 Serve soup sprinkled with parsley.

prep + cook time 6 hours 20 minutes
nutritional count per serving
3.9g total fat (0.8g saturated fat); 195 cal;
23.5g carbohydrate; 12.4g protein; 7.9g fiber

❄ suitable to freeze at the end of step 2.

ribollita

1 ham hock (2 pounds)
1 medium brown onion, chopped finely
2 stalks celery, trimmed, sliced thinly
1 large carrot, chopped finely
1 small fennel bulb, sliced thinly
3 cloves garlic, crushed
14½-ounce can diced tomatoes
2 sprigs fresh rosemary
½ teaspoon dried chili flakes
2 quarts water
12 ounces cavolo nero or kale,
  shredded coarsely
15-ounce can cannellini beans,
  rinsed, drained
½ cup coarsely chopped fresh basil
½ pound sourdough bread, crust removed
½ cup flaked parmesan cheese

1 Combine hock, onion, celery, carrot, fennel, garlic, undrained tomatoes, rosemary, chili, and the water in 4½-quart slow cooker. Cook, covered, on low, 8 hours.
2 Remove hock from cooker; add cavolo nero and beans to soup. Cook, covered, on high, about 20 minutes or until cavolo nero is wilted.
3 Meanwhile, when hock is cool enough to handle, remove meat from bone; shred coarsely. Discard skin, fat, and bone. Add meat and basil to soup; season to taste.
4 Break chunks of bread into serving bowls; top with soup and cheese.

prep + cook time 8 hours 45 minutes
nutritional count per serving
4.9g total fat (2.1g saturated fat); 191 cal; 18g carbohydrate; 15.1g protein; 7g fiber

tip Ribollita [ree-boh-lee-tah] literally means "reboiled." This famous Tuscan soup was originally made by reheating leftover minestrone or vegetable soup and adding chunks of bread, white beans, and other vegetables such as carrot, zucchini, spinach, and cavolo nero.

❄ suitable to freeze at the end of step 1.

pork and fennel soup

serves 6

1-pound piece pork neck
4 small potatoes, chopped coarsely
2 large fennel bulbs, chopped coarsely
  (see tip)
1 medium brown onion, chopped coarsely
2 cloves garlic, quartered
1 dried bay leaf
6 black peppercorns
1½ quarts water
2 cups chicken stock
½ cup light cream

1   Tie pork at 1-inch intervals with kitchen string. Combine the pork, potato, fennel, onion, garlic, bay leaf, peppercorns, the water, and stock in 4½-quart slow cooker. Cook, covered, on low, 6 hours.
2   Discard bay leaf. Transfer pork to medium bowl; remove string. Using two forks, shred pork coarsely.

3   Stand soup 10 minutes, then blend or process, in batches, until smooth. Return soup to cooker; stir in cream. Cook, covered, on high, until hot. Season to taste.
4   Serve soup topped with pork and reserved fennel fronds.

prep + cook time 6 hours 40 minutes
nutritional count per serving
16.2g total fat (8.4g saturated fat); 301 cal; 14.9g carbohydrate; 22g protein; 4.3g fiber

tip   Reserve some of the feathery fennel fronds to sprinkle over the soup at serving time.

❄   suitable to freeze at the end of step 1. Thaw and reheat soup, then shred pork.

pea and ham soup

serves 6

1 pound green split peas
1 tablespoon olive oil
1 large brown onion, chopped finely
3 cloves garlic, crushed
1 ham hock (2 pounds)
2 medium carrots, chopped finely
2 stalks celery, trimmed, chopped finely
4 fresh thyme sprigs
2 dried bay leaves
2 quarts water

serving suggestion Serve soup topped with coarsely chopped mint leaves, thinly sliced green onions (scallions), and Greek-style yogurt.

1 Rinse peas under cold water until water runs clear; drain.
2 Heat oil in large frying pan; cook onion and garlic, stirring, until onion softens. Place onion mixture into 4½-quart slow cooker; stir in peas and remaining ingredients. Cook, covered, on low, 8 hours.
3 Remove ham from cooker. When cool enough to handle, remove meat from bone; shred coarsely, return meat to slow cooker. Discard skin, fat, and bone. Season soup to taste.

prep + cook time 8 hours 20 minutes
nutritional count per serving
6.4g total fat (1.2g saturated fat); 363 cal; 43g carbohydrate; 27.3g protein; 11g fiber

❄ suitable to freeze at the end of step 2.

cuban black bean soup

1½ cups dried black turtle beans
1 ham hock (2 pounds)
2 tablespoons olive oil
1 large brown onion, chopped finely
1 medium red bell pepper, chopped finely
3 garlic cloves, crushed
3 teaspoons ground cumin
1 teaspoon dried chili flakes
14½-ounce canned crushed tomatoes
2 quarts water
1 tablespoon dried oregano leaves
1 teaspoon ground black pepper
2 tablespoons lime juice
1 large tomato, chopped finely
¼ cup coarsely chopped fresh coriander
(cilantro)

1 Place beans in medium bowl, cover with cold water; stand overnight.
2 Drain and rinse beans, place in medium saucepan, cover with cold water; bring to a boil. Boil, uncovered, 15 minutes; drain.
3 Meanwhile, preheat oven to 425°F.
4 Roast ham on oven tray for 30 minutes.
5 Heat oil in large frying pan; cook onion, red pepper, and garlic, stirring, until onion is soft. Add cumin and chili; cook, stirring, until fragrant.
6 Combine beans, ham, onion mixture, undrained tomatoes, the water, oregano, and pepper in 4½-quart slow cooker. Cook, covered, on low, 8 hours.
7 Remove ham from cooker. When cool enough to handle, remove meat from bone; shred coarsely. Discard skin, fat, and bone. Blend or process 2 cups soup mixture until smooth. Return meat to cooker with pureed soup, stir in juice and tomato; sprinkle with coriander. Season to taste.

prep + cook time 8 hours 55 minutes
(+ standing)
nutritional count per serving
18.1g total fat (2.9g saturated fat); 323 cal;
9.6g carbohydrate; 24.7g protein; 12.4g fiber

❄ suitable to freeze at the end of step 6.

asian noodle soup

2 pounds chicken necks
1 medium brown onion, chopped coarsely
1 stalk celery, trimmed, chopped coarsely
1 medium carrot, chopped coarsely
2 dried bay leaves
1 teaspoon black peppercorns
2½ quarts water
2 tablespoons tamari
1-inch piece fresh ginger, shredded finely
8 ounces dried ramen noodles
7 ounces firm Japanese tofu
1 tablespoon vegetable oil
3 ounces fresh shiitake mushrooms,
  sliced thinly
2 baby bok choy, chopped coarsely
2 ounces enoki mushrooms
2 green onions (scallions), sliced thinly

1   Combine chicken, onion, celery, carrot,
bay leaves, peppercorns, and the water in
4½-quart slow cooker. Cook, covered, on
low, 8 hours.
2   Strain stock through fine sieve into large
heatproof bowl; discard solids.
3   Return stock to cooker; add tamari and
ginger. Cook, uncovered, on high, about 20
minutes or until hot. Season to taste.
4   Meanwhile, cook noodles in medium
saucepan of boiling water until tender;
drain. Divide noodles into serving bowls.
Chop tofu into cubes.
5   Heat oil in same pan; cook shiitake
mushrooms, stirring, until browned all over.
Divide shiitake mushrooms, tofu, bok choy,
enoki mushrooms, green onions, and hot
stock between serving bowls.

prep + cook time 8 hours 50 minutes
nutritional count per serving
6.2g total fat (0.8g saturated fat); 242 cal;
32.4g carbohydrate; 11.4g protein; 5.1g fiber

 suitable to freeze at the end of step 1.

pumpkin soup

serves 6

2 tablespoons butter
1 tablespoon olive oil
1 large leek, sliced thinly
3¾-pound piece pumpkin,
  chopped coarsely
1 large potato, chopped coarsely
3 cups chicken stock
3 cups water
½ cup light cream
1 tablespoon finely chopped fresh chives

1   Heat butter and oil in large frying pan;
cook leek, stirring, until soft.
2   Combine leek mixture, pumpkin, potato,
stock, and the water in 4½-quart slow
cooker. Cook, covered, on low, 6 hours.
3   Cool soup 10 minutes. Blend or process
soup, in batches, until smooth. Return soup
to cooker. Cook, covered, on high, about 20
minutes or until hot. Stir in ⅓ cup of the
cream. Season to taste.
4   Serve soup topped with remaining cream
and chives.

prep + cook time 6 hours 30 minutes
nutritional count per serving
17.9g total fat (10.1g saturated fat); 305 cal;
24.8g carbohydrate; 9g protein; 5.1g fiber

❄   suitable to freeze at the end of step 2.

Stews & Casseroles

spicy tomato and saffron chicken casserole   serves 6

¼ cup all-purpose flour
2 tablespoons Moroccan seasoning
6 chicken thigh cutlets
1 tablespoon vegetable oil
1 large brown onion, sliced thickly
2 cloves garlic, crushed
1-inch piece fresh ginger, grated
1 fresh long red chili, sliced thinly
2 cups chicken stock
14½-ounce can diced tomatoes
¼ cup tomato paste
¼ teaspoon saffron threads

PRESERVED LEMON GREMOLATA
⅓ cup finely chopped fresh flat-leaf parsley
1 tablespoon thinly sliced preserved
  lemon rind
1 clove garlic, crushed

serving suggestion Serve casserole with
steamed rice or couscous.

1   Combine flour and 1 tablespoon of the
seasoning in small shallow bowl; toss
chicken in flour mixture to coat, shake off
excess. Heat half the oil in large frying pan;
cook chicken, in batches, until browned.
Transfer to 4½-quart slow cooker.
2   Heat remaining oil in same pan, add
onion, garlic, ginger, chili, and remaining
seasoning; cook, stirring, until onion
softens. Add ½ cup of the stock; cook,
stirring, until mixture boils.
3   Stir onion mixture into cooker with
remaining stock, undrained tomatoes,
paste, and saffron. Cook, covered, on low,
6 hours. Season to taste.
4   Make preserved lemon gremolata before
serving.
5   Sprinkle casserole with gremolata.

preserved lemon gremolata Combine
ingredients in small bowl.

prep + cook time 6 hours 25 minutes
nutritional count per serving
23.8g total fat (7.2g saturated fat); 364 cal;
10.2g carbohydrate; 26.5g protein; 2.5g fiber

tip   Preserved lemon is available at
delicatessens and some supermarkets.
Remove and discard the flesh, wash the
rind, then use it as the recipe directs.

❄ suitable to freeze at the end of step 3.

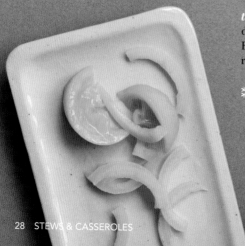

balsamic and port beef shanks

serves 6

1 tablespoon olive oil
3¾-pound piece beef shank,
  cut into 6 pieces
1 large red onion, sliced thickly
1 stalk celery, trimmed, sliced thickly
½ cup beef stock
½ cup port
¼ cup balsamic vinegar
14½-ounce canned diced tomatoes
2 sprigs fresh thyme
1 tablespoon light brown sugar
⅓ cup coarsely chopped fresh basil
2 teaspoons finely grated lemon rind
½ cup pitted black olives

serving suggestion Serve shanks with
risotto, mashed potato, or soft polenta.

1 Heat oil in large frying pan; cook beef, in
batches, until browned. Transfer to
4½-quart slow cooker. Add onion, celery,
stock, port, vinegar, undrained tomatoes,
thyme, and sugar to slow cooker; cook,
covered, on low, 8 hours.
2 Stir in basil, rind, and olives; season
to taste.
3 Serve beef with sauce.

prep + cook time 8 hours 20 minutes
nutritional count per serving
16.3g total fat (5.9g saturated fat); 413 cal;
12.1g carbohydrate; 48.2g protein; 1.9g fiber

tips Ask the butcher to cut the beef shank
into 6 equal pieces for you, or you could use
6 x 10 ounce pieces beef osso buco.
Dry red wine can be used instead of port.

❄ suitable to freeze at the end of step 1.

chili con carne

1 tablespoon olive oil
1 large brown onion, chopped finely
2 cloves garlic, crushed
1½ pounds ground beef
1 teaspoon ground cumin
1½ teaspoons dried chili flakes
1 cup beef stock
⅓ cup tomato paste
28-ounce can crushed tomatoes
1 tablespoon finely chopped fresh oregano
2 x 15-ounce cans kidney beans,
  rinsed, drained
½ cup loosely packed fresh coriander
  (cilantro) leaves
6 flour tortillas, warmed

1 Heat oil in large frying pan; cook onion and garlic, stirring, until onion softens. Add beef, cumin, and chili; cook, stirring, until browned. Transfer to 4½-quart slow cooker. Stir in stock, paste, undrained tomatoes, and oregano. Cook, covered, on low, 8 hours.
2 Add beans; cook, covered, on high, about 30 minutes or until hot. Season to taste.
3 Sprinkle chili con carne with coriander; serve with tortillas.

prep + cook time 8 hours 45 minutes
nutritional count per serving
14.8g total fat (5.4g saturated fat); 417 cal; 30.9g carbohydrate; 35.1g protein; 9.5g fiber

serving suggestion Serve chili con carne with steamed rice and a dollop of sour cream, plus a green leafy salad.

❄ suitable to freeze at the end of step 1.

corned beef with horseradish sauce

serves 6

3¼-pound piece corned beef (brisket or
  bottom round)
1 medium brown onion, chopped coarsely
1 medium carrot, chopped coarsely
1 stalk celery, trimmed, chopped coarsely
10 black peppercorns
1 tablespoon brown malt vinegar
1 teaspoon light brown sugar
2½ quarts water, approximately

HORSERADISH SAUCE
3 tablespoons butter
2 tablespoons all-purpose flour
2 cups hot milk
1 tablespoon horseradish cream
1 tablespoon coarsely chopped fresh
  flat-leaf parsley

1   Rinse beef under cold water; pat dry
with paper towels. Place beef, onion,
carrot, celery, peppercorns, vinegar, and
sugar in 4½-quart slow cooker. Add enough
of the water to barely cover beef. Cook,
covered, on low, 8 hours.
2   Make horseradish sauce just before
serving.
3   Remove beef from cooker; discard liquid
and vegetables.
4   Slice beef thickly; serve with horseradish
sauce.
horseradish sauce Melt butter in medium
saucepan, add flour; cook, stirring, 1
minute. Gradually add milk, stirring, until
sauce boils and thickens. Stir in horseradish
cream and parsley. Season to taste.

prep + cook time 8 hours 10 minutes
nutritional count per serving
26.1g total fat (13.9g saturated fat); 542 cal;
10.2g carbohydrate; 65.7g protein; 1.4g fiber

   not suitable to freeze.

serving suggestion A mixture of steamed seasonal vegetables makes a good accompaniment
to corned beef. Try baby potatoes, carrots, peas, or beans, squash, or zucchini.

artichokes with garlic anchovy crumbs serves 6 [as a starter]

6 medium globe artichokes
2 quarts water
2 cups chicken stock
2 tablespoons lemon juice
¼ cup olive oil

GARLIC ANCHOVY CRUMBS
1 tablespoon olive oil
6 anchovy filets, drained, chopped finely
3 cloves garlic, crushed
1½ cups stale breadcrumbs
1 tablespoon finely grated lemon rind
⅓ cup finely chopped fresh flat-leaf parsley
½ cup finely grated romano cheese

1   Remove and discard tough outer leaves from artichokes. Trim stems so artichoke bases sit flat. Using a small teaspoon, remove and discard hairy chokes from center of artichokes; rinse artichokes under cold water.
2   Pack artichokes tightly, upside down, into 4½-quart slow cooker; pour in the water, stock, and juice. Cook, covered, on low, 8 hours.
3   Make garlic anchovy crumbs before serving.
4   Remove artichokes with slotted spoon; drain well. Serve artichokes with olive oil and garlic anchovy crumbs for dipping.
garlic anchovy crumbs Heat oil in large frying pan; cook anchovy and garlic, stirring, until anchovy softens. Add breadcrumbs and rind; cook, stirring, until crumbs are browned lightly and crisp. Transfer to medium bowl; cool. Stir in parsley and cheese; season to taste.

prep + cook time 8 hours 35 minutes
nutritional count per serving
6.2g total fat (1.8g saturated fat); 155 cal; 13.9g carbohydrate; 9.5g protein; 2.3g fiber

serving suggestion Serve artichokes with some crusty bread and a green or tomato salad to make a main meal.

tip Artichoke leaves are pulled off the whole artichoke, one by one, and eaten by scraping against the teeth to extract the soft flesh at the base of each leaf. In this recipe we suggest dipping the leaves in a full-flavored olive oil and the flavored crumbs before eating.

❄ not suitable to freeze.

lamb, harissa, and chickpea casserole

serves 6

2½ pounds boned lamb shoulder,
  chopped coarsely
¼ cup all-purpose flour
1 tablespoon olive oil
1 medium red onion, sliced thinly
2 cloves garlic, crushed
¾-inch piece fresh ginger, grated
1 teaspoon ground allspice
1½ cups beef stock
2 tablespoons harissa paste
2 x 2-inch strips orange rind
2 x 15-ounce cans chickpeas,
  rinsed, drained
⅓ cup coarsely chopped fresh mint

1 Toss lamb in flour to coat; shake off excess. Heat half the oil in large frying pan; cook lamb, in batches, until browned. Transfer to 4½-quart slow cooker.

2 Heat remaining oil in same pan; cook onion, garlic, and ginger, stirring, until onion softens. Add allspice; cook, stirring, until fragrant. Add ½ cup of the stock; cook, stirring, until mixture boils.

3 Stir onion mixture into cooker with remaining stock, harissa, rind, and chickpeas. Cook, covered, on low, 7 hours.

4 Season to taste; sprinkle casserole with mint.

prep + cook time 7 hours 35 minutes
nutritional count per serving
23.1g total fat (9g saturated fat); 483 cal; 19.9g carbohydrate; 46.2g protein; 5.5g fiber

❄ suitable to freeze at the end of step 3.

serving suggestion Serve casserole with rice pilaf, steamed rice, or couscous.

veal and rosemary casserole

serves 6

2½ pounds boned veal shoulder,
  chopped coarsely
¼ cup all-purpose flour
1 tablespoon olive oil
1 medium brown onion, chopped coarsely
2 cloves garlic, crushed
½ cup dry red wine
2 medium carrots, chopped coarsely
2 stalks celery, trimmed, chopped coarsely
2 medium parsnips, chopped coarsely
2½ cups beef stock
3 sprigs fresh rosemary

1 Toss veal in flour to coat, shake off
excess. Heat half the oil in large frying pan;
cook veal, in batches, until browned.
Transfer to 4½-quart slow cooker.

2 Heat remaining oil in same pan; cook
onion and garlic, stirring, until onion
softens. Add wine; bring to a boil. Boil,
uncovered, until liquid reduces by half.
3 Stir onion mixture into cooker with
carrot, celery, parsnip, stock, and rosemary.
Cook, covered, on low, 8 hours. Season
to taste.

prep + cook time 8 hours 35 minutes
nutritional count per serving
8.6g total fat (2g saturated fat); 362 cal;
15.6g carbohydrate; 49.5g protein; 4.2g fiber

tip The butcher might have some good
stewing veal available, it's fine to use in this
recipe.

❄ suitable to freeze at the end of step 3.

serving suggestion Serve casserole with crusty bread or soft creamy polenta.

italian beef casserole

2½ pounds beef blade steak,
  chopped coarsely
¼ cup all-purpose flour
1 tablespoon olive oil
1 large brown onion, chopped coarsely
2 cloves garlic, crushed
½ teaspoon dried chili flakes
½ cup dry red wine
14½-ounce can diced tomatoes
¼ cup tomato paste
2½ cups beef stock
2 dried bay leaves
1 large red bell pepper, chopped coarsely
1 tablespoon finely chopped fresh oregano
⅓ cup coarsely chopped fresh basil
1 large zucchini, halved lengthways,
  sliced thickly
6 ounces swiss brown mushrooms, halved
⅓ cup loosely packed fresh basil leaves

1 Toss beef in flour to coat, shake off excess. Heat half the oil in large frying pan; cook beef, in batches, until browned. Transfer to 4½-quart slow cooker.
2 Heat remaining oil in same pan; cook onion, garlic, and chili, stirring, until onion softens. Add wine; bring to a boil. Boil, uncovered, until liquid reduces by half.
3 Stir onion mixture into cooker with undrained tomatoes, paste, stock, bay leaves, peppers, oregano, and the chopped basil. Cook, covered, on low, 8 hours.
4 Add zucchini and mushrooms to cooker for last 30 minutes of cooking time. Discard bay leaves. Season to taste.
5 Sprinkle casserole with basil leaves to serve.

prep + cook time 8 hours 30 minutes
nutritional count per serving
16.8g total fat (6.2g saturated fat); 414 cal; 12.5g carbohydrate; 47.6g protein; 4g fiber

❄ suitable to freeze at the end of step 3.

serving suggestion Serve casserole with creamy polenta, mashed potatoes, or pasta.

seafood in romesco sauce

serves 6

2 pounds cleaned whole baby octopus
28-ounce can crushed tomatoes
4 cloves garlic, crushed
1 teaspoon dried chili flakes
2 teaspoons smoked paprika
2 medium red bell peppers, sliced thinly
2 tablespoons red wine vinegar
1 pound uncooked medium king prawns
1 pound cleaned mussels
½ cup ground almonds
½ cup coarsely chopped fresh flat-leaf
    parsley
⅓ cup coarsely chopped fresh oregano

1 Combine octopus, undrained tomatoes, garlic, chili, paprika, peppers, and vinegar in 4½-quart slow cooker; cook, covered, on low, 4 hours.
2 Meanwhile, shell and devein prawns, leaving tails intact. Add prawns, mussels, and ground almonds to cooker; cook, covered, stirring occasionally, on high, about 20 minutes or until prawns change color and mussels open (discard any that do not).
3 Serve sprinkled with herbs.

prep + cook time 4 hours 45 minutes
nutritional count per serving
9.5g total fat (1.2g saturated fat); 361 cal;
9.5g carbohydrate; 57.1g protein; 3.7g fiber

tip Packets of ground almonds are sometimes sold as almond meal. They are available from health food stores and most major supermarkets.

❄ not suitable to freeze.

serving suggestion Serve with steamed rice or crusty bread.

rabbit with sweet potato and sage

serves 6

3¼-pound rabbit
12 baby brown or pearl onions
1 medium white or orange sweet potato, chopped coarsely
2 medium potatoes, chopped coarsely
1 cup verjuice or dry white wine
1 cup chicken stock
2 cloves garlic, sliced thinly
¼ cup loosely packed fresh sage leaves

1 Cut rabbit into six serving-sized pieces. Peel onions, leaving root ends intact.
2 Combine rabbit, onion, and remaining ingredients in 4½-quart slow cooker; cook, covered, on low, 6 hours. Season to taste.
3 Serve rabbit and vegetables drizzled with broth.

prep + cook time 6 hours 20 minutes
nutritional count per serving
4.6g total fat (1.7g saturated fat); 266 cal; 21.6g carbohydrate; 32.6g protein; 3g fiber

tips Ask the butcher to cut the rabbit into pieces for you.
Verjuice is available in delis and supermarkets; it's usually found in the vinegar aisle. It's made from unripe grapes and has a slightly acidic taste.

❄ not suitable to freeze.

serving suggestion Serve with crusty bread and steamed beans or broccoli.

beef, date, and spinach tagine

serves 6

2½ pounds beef blade steak, chopped coarsely
¼ cup all-purpose flour
1 tablespoon olive oil
1 large red onion, chopped finely
2 cloves garlic, crushed
1 teaspoon ground cinnamon
1 teaspoon ground cumin
½ teaspoon ground ginger
½ teaspoon ground turmeric
¼ teaspoon saffron threads
1 cup beef stock
14½-ounce can diced tomatoes
¾ cup pitted dried dates
10 ounces spinach, shredded coarsely
1 tablespoon thinly sliced preserved lemon rind
⅓ cup coarsely chopped roasted unsalted pistachios

1 Toss beef in flour to coat, shake off excess.
Heat half the oil in large frying pan; cook beef, in batches, until browned. Transfer to 4½-quart slow cooker.
2 Heat remaining oil in same pan; cook onion and garlic, stirring, until onion softens. Add spices; cook, stirring, until fragrant. Add ½ cup of the stock; cook, stirring, until mixture boils.
3 Transfer onion mixture to cooker with remaining stock and undrained tomatoes; stir to combine. Cook, covered, on low, 8 hours.
4 Add dates, spinach, and half the preserved lemon rind; cook, covered, on high, about 10 minutes or until spinach wilts. Season to taste.
5 Sprinkle tagine with nuts and remaining preserved lemon rind.

prep + cook time 8 hours 35 minutes
nutritional count per serving
20.4g total fat (6.5g saturated fat); 473 cal; 22g carbohydrate; 47.5g protein; 5.6g fiber

serving suggestion Serve tagine with steamed couscous or rice.

tips Beef shin or chuck steak could also be used.
Preserved lemon is available at delis and some supermarkets. Remove and discard the lemon flesh, wash the rind, then use it as the recipe directs.

❄ suitable to freeze at the end of step 3.

best-ever bolognese sauce

serves 6

1 tablespoon olive oil
4-ounce piece prosciutto, chopped finely
2 medium brown onions, chopped finely
1 large carrot, chopped finely
2 stalks celery, trimmed, chopped finely
2 cloves garlic, crushed
1 pound ground veal
1 pound ground pork
1 cup dry red wine
1½ cups beef stock
¼ cup tomato paste
2 pounds ripe tomatoes, peeled, seeded, chopped coarsely
⅓ cup finely chopped fresh basil
2 tablespoons finely chopped fresh oregano

1 Heat half the oil in large frying pan; cook prosciutto, stirring, until crisp. Add onion, carrot, celery, and garlic; cook, stirring, until vegetables soften. Transfer to 4½-quart slow cooker.
2 Heat remaining oil in same pan; cook meat, stirring, until browned. Add wine; bring to a boil. Stir meat mixture into cooker with stock, paste, and tomatoes; cook, covered, on low, 10 hours.
3 Stir in herbs; cook, covered, on high, 10 minutes. Season to taste.

prep + cook time 10 hours 40 minutes
nutritional count per serving
16.3g total fat (5.4g saturated fat); 377 cal; 7.4g carbohydrate; 41.7g protein; 3.5g fiber

serving suggestion Serve bolognese with spaghetti or your favorite pasta; top with shaved parmesan cheese.

tips Prosciutto can be replaced with bacon. Fresh tomatoes can be replaced with a 28-ounce can of diced tomatoes.

❄ suitable to freeze at the end of step 2.

chicken cacciatore

2 tablespoons olive oil
12 chicken drumsticks, skin removed
1 medium brown onion, sliced thickly
3 cloves garlic, crushed
3 drained anchovy filets, crushed
½ cup dry white wine
⅓ cup chicken stock
⅓ cup tomato pasta sauce
2 tablespoons tomato paste
2 teaspoons finely chopped fresh basil
1 teaspoon superfine sugar
⅓ cup pitted black olives, halved
1 tablespoon finely chopped fresh
    flat-leaf parsley

serving suggestion Serve cacciatore with
creamy mashed potatoes or crusty bread.

1 Heat oil in large frying pan; cook
chicken, in batches, until browned all over.
Transfer chicken to 4½-quart slow cooker.
2 Cook onion, garlic, and anchovy in same
pan, stirring, until onion softens. Add wine;
bring to a boil. Boil, uncovered, until
reduced by half; stir into cooker with stock,
sauce, paste, basil, and sugar. Cook,
covered, on low, 6 hours.
3 Stir in olives and parsley; season
to taste.

prep + cook time 6 hours 25 minutes
nutritional count per serving
18.5g total fat (4.4g saturated fat); 359 cal;
6.9g carbohydrate; 37.2g protein; 1.3g fiber

tip Use a plain (unflavored) tomato-based
sauce suitable for serving over pasta. These
sauces can be bought in cans and jars and
are often labeled "sugo" or "passata".

❄ suitable to freeze at the end of step 2.

moroccan lamb with sweet potato and raisins serves 6

2 tablespoons olive oil
2½ pounds boned lamb shoulder,
    chopped coarsely
1 large brown onion, sliced thickly
4 cloves garlic, crushed
2 tablespoons ras el hanout
2 cups chicken stock
½ cup water
1 tablespoon honey
2 medium sweet potatoes,
    chopped coarsely
15-ounce can chickpeas,
    rinsed, drained
1 cinnamon stick
3 cardamom pods, bruised
⅓ cup raisins, halved
½ cup loosely packed fresh coriander
    (cilantro) leaves
⅓ cup coarsely chopped blanched
    almonds, roasted

1 Heat half the oil in large frying pan; cook lamb, in batches, until browned all over. Remove from pan. Heat remaining oil in same pan; cook onion and garlic, stirring, until onion is soft. Add ras el hanout; cook, stirring, until fragrant. Remove from heat; stir in stock, the water and honey.
2 Place potatoes in 4½-quart slow cooker; stir in chickpeas, cinnamon, cardamom, lamb, and onion mixture. Cook, covered, on low, 6 hours. Season to taste.
3 Stir in raisins and coriander; sprinkle with nuts to serve.

prep + cook time 6 hours 25 minutes
nutritional count per serving
30.5g total fat (9.7g saturated fat); 614 cal; 34.9g carbohydrate; 47.2g protein; 6.3g fiber

tip Ras el hanout is a blend of Moroccan spices available in delis and specialty food stores. If you can't find it, use a Moroccan seasoning available in supermarkets.

❄ suitable to freeze at the end of step 2.

serving suggestion Serve tagine with buttered couscous and steamed baby green beans.

beef ribs with stout and caramelized onion   serves 6

1 tablespoon olive oil
5 pounds beef shortribs on the bone
2 large brown onions, sliced thinly
1 tablespoon light brown sugar
1 tablespoon balsamic vinegar
¼ cup water
3 medium carrots, sliced thickly
14½-ounce can diced tomatoes
5 sprigs fresh thyme
1 tablespoon Dijon mustard
1 cup beef stock
1 cup stout beer

serving suggestion Serve ribs with steamed rice and a green leafy salad.

1 Heat half the oil in large frying pan; cook ribs, in batches, until browned. Remove from pan.
2 Heat remaining oil in large frying pan; cook onion, stirring, until soft. Add sugar, vinegar, and the water; cook, stirring occasionally, about 10 minutes or until onion caramelizes.
3 Transfer onion mixture to 4½-quart slow cooker; stir in carrot, undrained tomatoes, thyme, mustard, stock, and stout. Add ribs, turn to coat in sauce mixture. Cook, covered, on low, 8 hours. Season to taste.
4 Cut ribs into serving-sized pieces; serve with the sauce.

prep + cook time 8 hours 45 minutes
nutritional count per serving
21.4g total fat (8.1g saturated fat); 533 cal; 12g carbohydrate; 67.2g protein; 3.5g fiber

tips Stout is a strong-flavored, dark-colored type of beer originally from Britain. It is made with roasted barley, giving it its characteristic dark color and bittersweet, almost coffee-like, flavor.

❄ suitable to freeze at the end of step 3.

chili and brandy beef with white beans

serves 6

6 shallots
2½ pounds beef brisket, chopped coarsely
1 fresh long red chili, chopped finely
2 cloves garlic, crushed
3 medium plum tomatoes,
  chopped coarsely
2 tablespoons tomato paste
1 cup beef stock
¼ cup brandy
15-ounce can cannellini beans,
  rinsed, drained
⅓ cup coarsely chopped fresh flat-leaf
  parsley

1 Peel shallots, leaving root ends intact;
cut shallots in half lengthwise.
2 Combine shallot, beef, chili, garlic,
tomato, paste, stock, and brandy in
4½-quart slow cooker; cook, covered,
on low, 8 hours.

3 Add beans; cook, covered, on high,
about 20 minutes or until hot. Stir in
parsley; season to taste.

prep + cook time 8 hours 25 minutes
nutritional count per serving
12.1g total fat (5.1g saturated fat); 329 cal;
3.6g carbohydrate; 45g protein; 2.2g fiber

tips For a slightly richer color and flavor,
brown the beef in a little oil in a frying pan
before adding it to the slow cooker.
Any type of white beans can be used; navy,
great northern, or haricot are all good
choices.
Beef brisket is an economical cut of meat;
ask the butcher to trim the fat away and to
chop the meat for you.

❄ suitable to freeze at the end of step 2.

serving suggestion This recipe is very hearty, a simple green salad or crusty bread would go
well as an accompaniment.

coq au vin

20 spring onions or large scallions
2 tablespoons olive oil
6 strips bacon, sliced thinly
14 ounces button mushrooms
2 cloves garlic, crushed
3¾-pound whole chicken
2 cups dry red wine
2 medium carrots, chopped coarsely
3 dried bay leaves
4 sprigs fresh thyme
2 sprigs fresh rosemary
1½ cups chicken stock
¼ cup tomato paste
¼ cup corn starch
2 tablespoons water

1 Trim green ends from onions, leaving about 1½ inches of stem attached; trim roots leaving onions intact. Heat half the oil in large frying pan; cook onions, stirring, until browned all over, remove from pan. Add bacon, mushrooms, and garlic to same pan; cook, stirring, until bacon is crisp, remove from pan.
2 Cut chicken into 12 pieces. Heat remaining oil in same pan; cook chicken, in batches, until browned all over; drain on paper towels. Add wine to same pan; bring to a boil, stirring.
3 Place chicken in 4½-quart slow cooker with onions, bacon, and mushroom mixture, carrot, herbs, stock, wine mixture, and paste. Cook, covered, on low, 7 hours.
4 Stir in blended corn starch and the water; cook, covered, on high, about 20 minutes or until sauce thickens slightly. Season to taste.

prep + cook time 8 hours
nutritional count per serving
39.6g total fat (11.7g saturated fat); 658 cal; 12.3g carbohydrate; 47.8g protein; 5.1g fiber

tips Use chicken pieces if you prefer, such as 6 thighs and 6 drumsticks, or ask your butcher to cut the chicken into 12 serving pieces for you. Use shallots instead of spring onions, if you like.

 not suitable to freeze.

serving suggestion Serve coq au vin over creamy mashed potatoes drizzled with some of the sauce; accompany with a green salad.

pickled pork

serves 6

6½-pound pickled pork front quarter
  pork leg, or pickled hocks
2 tablespoons brown malt vinegar
2 dried bay leaves
1 teaspoon black peppercorns
2 tablespoons dark brown sugar
1½ quarts water, approximately

1   Place pork, vinegar, bay leaves,
peppercorns, and sugar in 4½-quart slow
cooker; add enough of the water to barely
cover pork. Cook, covered, on low, 8 hours.
2   Carefully remove pork from cooking
liquid; cover, stand 10 minutes before
slicing. Discard cooking liquid.

prep + cook time 8 hours 10 minutes
nutritional count per serving
27.8g total fat (10.7g saturated fat); 670 cal;
4.2g carbohydrate; 100.7g protein; 0g fiber

tip Pickled pork leg can be found in
German butcher shops or ordered online.
You can substitute an equal amount of
pickled pork hocks, which are more readily
available. You might need to order this from
the butcher in advance.

❄   not suitable to freeze.

serving suggestions Pickled pork is delicious served hot with mashed potatoes, wilted
cabbage, and mustard, or it can be served cold (like ham) with potato salad or coleslaw.

honey and balsamic braised pork

serves 6

2 tablespoons olive oil
2½-pound piece pork neck
9 shallots, halved
1½ cups chicken stock
⅓ cup white balsamic vinegar
¼ cup honey
6 cloves garlic, peeled
2 sprigs fresh rosemary
1 cup pitted green olives

1 Heat oil in large frying pan; cook pork until browned all over. Remove from pan.
2 Add shallots to same pan; cook, stirring, until browned all over. Add stock, vinegar, and honey; bring to a boil.

3 Place garlic and rosemary in 4½-quart slow cooker; top with pork. Pour shallot mixture over; cook, covered, on low, 7 hours.
4 Add olives; cook, covered, on low, 30 minutes. Season to taste.
5 Remove pork; stand, covered, 10 minutes before slicing. Serve pork drizzled with sauce.

prep + cook time 8 hours
nutritional count per serving
23.6g total fat (6.5g saturated fat); 471 cal; 20g carbohydrate; 44g protein; 1.1g fiber

serving suggestion Serve pork with mashed potatoes or soft creamy polenta, plus some wilted shredded cabbage.

❄ suitable to freeze at the end of step 3.

chinese chicken hot pot

serves 6

3¾-pound whole chicken
1 quart water
1 quart chicken stock
2 cups Chinese cooking wine
½ cup light soy sauce
⅓ cup oyster sauce
⅓ cup firmly packed light brown sugar
4 cloves garlic, bruised
2¼-inch piece fresh ginger,
  sliced thinly
3 star anise
1 teaspoon five-spice powder
2 fresh long red chilies, halved lengthways
1 pound baby bok choy, chopped coarsely
⅓ cup coarsely chopped fresh coriander
  (cilantro)
1 fresh long red chili, extra, sliced thinly

1 Rinse chicken under cold water; pat dry, inside and out, with paper towels. Combine the water, stock, cooking wine, sauces, sugar, garlic, ginger, spices, and chili in 4½-quart slow cooker. Add chicken; cook, covered, on low, 8 hours.

2 Remove chicken; strain broth through fine sieve into large bowl. Discard solids. Cover chicken to keep warm. Return broth to cooker. Add bok choy to cooker; cook, covered, on high, about 5 minutes or until tender.

3 Cut chicken into 6 pieces; serve with bok choy, drizzle with the broth. Sprinkle with coriander and extra chili.

prep + cook time 8 hours 20 minutes
nutritional count per serving
25.2g total fat (7.9g saturated fat); 487 cal; 20.8g carbohydrate; 34.8g protein; 1.7g fiber

tip Chinese cooking wine is also known as Chinese rice wine and shao hsing wine. Dry sherry can be used instead.

❄ suitable to freeze at the end of step 1.

serving suggestion Serve with steamed fresh rice noodles or rice.

creamy turkey stew with mustard

serves 8

4 turkey drumsticks, skin removed
2 tablespoons olive oil
12 ounces button mushrooms
2 medium leeks, sliced thickly
4 strips bacon, chopped coarsely
2 cloves garlic, crushed
2 tablespoons all-purpose flour
1 cup chicken stock
½ cup dry white wine
2 tablespoons whole grain mustard
6 sprigs fresh lemon thyme
½ cup cream
2 teaspoons fresh lemon thyme leaves

1   Using sharp heavy knife, cut turkey meat from bones, chop meat coarsely; discard bones.

serving suggestion Serve stew with mashed potatoes and steamed green beans.

2   Heat oil in large frying pan; cook turkey, in batches, until browned all over. Transfer turkey to 4½-quart slow cooker.
3   Add mushrooms, leek, bacon, and garlic to same pan; cook, stirring, until leek softens. Add flour; cook, stirring, 1 minute. Stir in stock, wine, mustard, and thyme sprigs; bring to a boil. Boil, uncovered, 2 minutes. Remove from heat; stir in cream. Transfer mushroom mixture to cooker. Cook, covered, on low, 2 hours.
4   Season to taste; sprinkle with thyme leaves.

prep + cook time 2 hours 30 minutes
nutritional count per serving
23.2g total fat (8.8g saturated fat); 458 cal; 5.3g carbohydrate; 53.2g protein; 3.1g fiber

❆   not suitable to freeze.

hungarian veal goulash

serves 6

2 pounds boned veal shoulder,
chopped coarsely
¼ cup all-purpose flour
1 tablespoon sweet paprika
2 teaspoons caraway seeds
½ teaspoon cayenne pepper
2 tablespoons olive oil
1 tablespoon butter
1 large brown onion, chopped coarsely
2 cloves garlic, crushed
2 tablespoons tomato paste
1½ cups beef stock
14½-ounce can crushed tomatoes
3 small potatoes, quartered
2 medium carrots, chopped coarsely
½ cup sour cream
½ cup coarsely chopped fresh
flat-leaf parsley

serving suggestion Serve goulash
with crusty bread, rice, or pasta.

1 Toss veal in combined flour and spices to
coat; shake away excess flour. Heat half the
oil and half the butter in large frying pan;
cook veal, in batches, until browned all over.
Transfer to 4½-quart slow cooker.
2 Heat remaining oil and butter in same
pan; cook onion and garlic, stirring, until
onion is soft. Stir in paste and stock; bring to
a boil. Stir into cooker with undrained
tomatoes, potato, and carrot; cook, covered,
on low, 8 hours.
3 Season to taste; dollop with sour cream
and sprinkle with parsley to serve.

prep + cook time 8 hours 30 minutes
nutritional count per serving
20.7g total fat (8.7g saturated fat); 439 cal;
18.4g carbohydrate; 42.6g protein; 4.1g fiber

tip The butcher might have some good
stewing veal available; it's fine to use in this
recipe.

❄ suitable to freeze at the end of step 2.

simple beef and vegetable casserole

serves 6

2½ pounds beef chuck steak,
  chopped coarsely
⅓ cup all-purpose flour
¼ cup olive oil
2 medium brown onions, cut into
  thick wedges
2 medium carrots, chopped coarsely
2 stalks celery, trimmed, chopped coarsely
1 medium parsnip, chopped coarsely
1 medium rutabaga, chopped coarsely
3 cloves garlic, crushed
¼ cup tomato paste
14½-ounce canned crushed tomatoes
1 cup beef stock
2 dried bay leaves
10 sprigs fresh thyme

1 Coat beef in flour; shake off excess. Heat 2 tablespoons of the oil in large frying pan; cook beef, in batches, until browned all over. Transfer beef to 4½-quart slow cooker.
2 Heat remaining oil in same pan; cook onion, carrot, celery, parsnip, rutabaga, and garlic; stirring, until onion softens. Add paste; cook, stirring, 1 minute. Remove from heat; stir in undrained tomatoes and stock.
3 Stir vegetable mixture and bay leaves into cooker; add thyme. Cook, covered, on low, 8 hours. Discard thyme and bay leaves; season to taste.

prep + cook time 8 hours 30 minutes
nutritional count per serving
18.7g total fat (5.2g saturated fat); 437 cal; 19.3g carbohydrate; 44.9g protein; 5.9g fiber

serving suggestion Serve casserole with crusty bread.

tips Use whatever vegetables you like: turnip, celeriac, Jerusalem artichokes are all good choices.
Boneless beef shin can be used instead of chuck steak.

❄ suitable to freeze at the end of step 2.

ratatouille

serves 6

2 tablespoons olive oil
1 large red onion, chopped coarsely
3 cloves garlic, crushed
½ cup loosely packed fresh basil leaves
2 tablespoons tomato paste
3 cups tomato pasta sauce
2 teaspoons superfine sugar
1 large eggplant, chopped coarsely
2 medium red bell peppers,
   chopped coarsely
2 large zucchinis, chopped coarsely
1 medium green bell pepper,
   chopped coarsely

1 Heat oil in large frying pan; cook onion, garlic, and half the basil, stirring, until onion softens. Add paste; cook, stirring, 1 minute. Remove from heat, stir in pasta sauce and sugar.

2 Place vegetables and sauce mixture into 4½-quart slow cooker. Cook, covered, on low, 4 hours. Season to taste.

3 Serve ratatouille sprinkled with remaining basil.

prep + cook time 4 hours 20 minutes
nutritional count per serving
7.5g total fat (1g saturated fat); 192 cal; 22.1g carbohydrate; 5.5g protein; 7g fiber

tip Use a plain (unflavored) tomato-based sauce suitable for serving over pasta. These sauces can be bought in cans and jars and are often labeled "sugo" or "passata".

❄ suitable to freeze at the end of step 2, although it's much better right after cooking.

serving suggestion Serve ratatouille with soft creamy polenta.

veal with parsley and capers

serves 6

2½ pounds boned veal shoulder,
  chopped coarsely
⅓ cup all-purpose flour
¼ cup olive oil
8 shallots
12 ounces button mushrooms
1 cup dry white wine
4 beef marrow bones
1 cup chicken stock
4 dried bay leaves
1 cup frozen peas, thawed
1 cup coarsely chopped fresh
  flat-leaf parsley
1 tablespoon rinsed, drained baby capers
2 teaspoons finely grated lemon rind
2 cloves garlic, chopped finely

serving suggestion Serve with creamy
mashed potatoes and a green leafy salad.

1 Coat veal in flour; shake off excess. Heat
2 tablespoons of the oil in large frying pan;
cook veal, in batches, until browned all
over. Transfer veal to 4½-quart slow cooker.
2 Meanwhile, peel shallots, leave roots
intact. Heat remaining oil in same pan; cook
shallots and mushrooms, stirring, until
browned. Add wine, bring to a boil; boil,
uncovered, until reduced by half.
3 Add marrow bones, stock, bay leaves,
and shallot mixture to cooker. Cook,
covered, on low, 6 hours.
4 Discard marrow bones and bay leaves.
Stir in peas, parsley, capers, rind, and garlic;
season to taste.

prep + cook time 6 hours 30 minutes
nutritional count per serving
16.5g total fat (3.4g saturated fat); 434 cal;
9.1g carbohydrate; 53.4g protein; 4g fiber

tip The butcher might have some good
stewing veal available, it's fine to use in this
recipe.

❄ not suitable to freeze.

osso buco with mixed mushrooms

serves 6

6 large pieces beef osso buco (3 ¾ pounds)
¼ cup all-purpose flour
2 tablespoons olive oil
1 large brown onion, chopped coarsely
1 cup marsala
1½ cups beef stock
¼ cup Worcestershire sauce
2 tablespoons whole grain mustard
2 sprigs fresh rosemary
6 ounces cremini mushrooms,
  sliced thickly
5 ounces portabello mushrooms,
  cut into 8 wedges
5 ounces oyster mushrooms,
  chopped coarsely
½ cup light cream
¼ cup powdered gravy mix
2 tablespoons water
½ cup coarsely chopped fresh
  flat-leaf parsley

1 Coat beef all over in flour, shake off excess. Heat half the oil in large frying pan; cook beef, in batches, until browned all over. Remove from pan.
2 Heat remaining oil in same pan; cook onion, stirring, until onion softens. Add marsala; bring to a boil. Add onion mixture to 4½-quart slow cooker; stir in stock, sauce, mustard, and rosemary. Place beef in cooker, fitting pieces upright and tightly packed in a single layer. Add mushrooms to cooker. Cook, covered, on low, 8 hours.
3 Carefully remove beef from cooker; cover to keep warm. Add cream and combined gravy powder and the water to cooker; cook, covered, on high, 10 minutes or until mixture thickens slightly. Stir in parsley; season to taste.
4 Serve beef with mushroom sauce.

prep + cook time 8 hours 50 minutes
nutritional count per serving
16.5g total fat (7.1g saturated fat); 455 cal;
17.4g carbohydrate; 45.5g protein; 3.7g fiber

serving suggestion Serve osso buco with a mash—potato, celeriac, or sweet potato are all good—and a green leafy salad.

tips Ask the butcher for either veal or beef shin (osso buco)—veal will be smaller than beef, in which case you will need about 12 pieces to serve six people. You can use a mixture of mushrooms as we have, or just one variety with a good robust flavor—you need a total of 1 pound.

❄ not suitable to freeze.

red wine, beef, and mushroom stew

serves 6

16 spring onions or large scallions
2 tablespoons olive oil
12 ounces button mushrooms
4 strips bacon, chopped coarsely
3 cloves garlic, crushed
1 cup dry red wine
¼ cup tomato paste
½ teaspoon superfine sugar
2½ pounds boneless beef shin,
    chopped coarsely
2 medium fennel bulbs, sliced thickly
⅓ cup coarsely chopped fresh
    flat-leaf parsley

1 Trim green ends from onions, leaving about 3 inches of stems attached; trim roots. Heat oil in large frying pan; cook onions, mushrooms, bacon, and garlic, stirring, until onion softens. Stir in wine, paste, and sugar; bring to a boil; boil, uncovered, 2 minutes.
2 Place beef, fennel, and onion mixture in 4½-quart slow cooker. Cook, covered, on low, 8 hours.
3 Stir in parsley; season to taste.

prep + cook time 8 hours 25 minutes
nutritional count per serving
21.3g total fat (6.8g saturated fat); 467 cal; 6.3g carbohydrate; 53.1g protein; 5.2g fiber

tip Chuck steak or any stewing steak can be used instead of beef shin.

❄ not suitable to freeze.

serving suggestion Serve stew over creamy polenta or mashed potatoes; accompany with steamed green beans.

creamy potato bake

serves 8 [as an accompaniment]

1 tablespoon olive oil
2 medium leeks, sliced thinly
4 strips bacon, chopped finely
2 tablespoons coarsely chopped fresh
  flat-leaf parsley
3¼ pounds potatoes, sliced thinly
2 cups light cream
¼ cup milk
1 tablespoon dijon mustard
1½-ounce packet dried chicken noodle
  soup mix
½ cup coarsely grated white
  cheddar cheese
½ cup finely grated parmesan cheese

1   Heat oil in large frying pan; cook leek and bacon, stirring, until leek softens. Remove from heat; stir in parsley.

2   Layer one third of the potato in 4½-quart slow cooker; top with half the leek mixture. Repeat layering with remaining potato and leek, finishing with potato layer.
3   Combine cream, milk, mustard, and soup mix in large pitcher, pour over potatoes; sprinkle with combined cheeses. Cook, covered, on low, 6 hours.

prep + cook time 6 hours 25 minutes
nutritional count per serving
38.7g total fat (22.7g saturated fat); 540 cal; 29.5g carbohydrate; 17.3g protein; 4.3g fiber

tip It's important to slice the potatoes thinly; a mandolin or V-slicer makes the job quick and easy.

❄ not suitable to freeze.

serving suggestion Serve spoonfuls of the bake with a green leafy salad as a light meal, or serve the bake as an accompaniment to a main course.

braised beef cheeks in stout

serves 6

2 tablespoons olive oil
6 beef cheeks (3¼ pounds)
12 shallots
2 cloves garlic, crushed
1 cup beef stock
2 medium carrots, chopped coarsely
9 ounces portabello mushrooms,
  chopped coarsely
3 cups stout beer
2 tablespoons dark brown sugar
2 sprigs fresh rosemary
¼ cup corn starch
2 tablespoons water

1 Heat half the oil in large frying pan; cook beef, in batches, until browned all over. Transfer to 4½-quart slow cooker.
2 Meanwhile, peel shallots, trim roots, leaving shallots whole; halve shallots lengthwise.
3 Heat remaining oil in same pan; cook shallots and garlic, stirring, until shallots are browned lightly. Add stock; bring to a boil. Stir shallot mixture into cooker with carrot, mushrooms, stout, sugar, and rosemary. Cook, covered, on low, 9 hours.
4 Carefully remove beef from cooker; cover to keep warm. Stir blended corn starch and the water into cooker; cook, covered, on high, about 15 minutes or until thickened slightly. Season to taste.
5 Serve beef with sauce.

prep + cook time 9 hours 45 minutes
nutritional count per serving
26.2g total fat (9.4g saturated fat); 580 cal; 16.8g carbohydrate; 55.7g protein; 2.8g fiber

tips Beef cheeks are available from most butchers, but you might need to order them in advance. Substitute beef shin, chuck, or blade steak if cheeks are unavailable. Stout is a strong-flavored, dark-colored beer made from barley.

 not suitable to freeze.

serving suggestion Serve beef with creamy mashed potatoes or colcannon (mashed potatoes with cabbage).

honey soy lamb chops

serves 6

¼ cup low-sodium soy sauce
¼ cup honey
3 cloves garlic, crushed
1 teaspoon sesame oil
2 large red onions, cut into thick wedges
6 lamb forequarter chops (2½ pounds)
6 sprigs fresh rosemary
1 tablespoon butter, melted
1 tablespoon all-purpose flour

1 Combine sauce, honey, garlic, and oil in small pitcher.
2 Place onion in 4½-quart slow cooker; top with lamb, soy sauce mixture, and rosemary. Cook, covered, on low, 6 hours.
3 Discard rosemary, remove lamb from cooker; cover to keep warm.

4 Combine butter and flour in small bowl; stir into cooker. Cook, covered, on high, about 25 minutes or until sauce thickens; season to taste. Strain sauce through fine sieve into medium heatproof pitcher; discard onion.
5 Serve lamb drizzled with sauce.

prep + cook time 6 hours
nutritional count per serving
16.9g total fat (8.2g saturated fat); 380cal; 19.5g carbohydrate; 36.2g protein; 1.6g fiber

❄ suitable to freeze at the end of step 2.

serving suggestion Steamed potatoes, baby peas, and carrots make a great accompaniment.

lamb and potato stew with spinach

serves 6

3 medium potatoes, unpeeled, cut into
  thick wedges
2 large brown onions, sliced thickly
2 large carrots, sliced thickly
4 cloves garlic, sliced thinly
2½ pounds boned lamb leg,
  chopped coarsely
1½ cups chicken stock
1⅔ cups canned tomato puree
4 sprigs fresh thyme
2 ounces baby spinach leaves

1 Place potatoes, onion, carrot, garlic, and
lamb in 4½-quart slow cooker; stir in stock,
puree, and thyme. Cook, covered, on low, 6
hours.
2 Discard thyme. Stir in spinach leaves;
season to taste.

prep + cook time 6 hours 20 minutes
nutritional count per serving
11.4g total fat (4.9g saturated fat); 401 cal;
21.6g carbohydrate; 49.6g protein; 5.9g fiber

❄ not suitable to freeze.

serving suggestion Serve stew with crusty bread and steamed green vegetables.

chili beans with tomato sauce

serves 6

1 tablespoon olive oil
6 strips bacon, chopped finely
1 stalk celery, trimmed, chopped finely
1 small brown onion, chopped finely
1 small carrot, chopped finely
1 fresh long red chili, chopped finely
¼ cup tomato paste
3 cups bottled tomato pasta sauce
¾ cup chicken stock
2 teaspoons superfine sugar
2 x 15-ounce canned cannellini beans,
  rinsed, drained
¼ cup coarsely chopped fresh flat-leaf
  parsley

1 Heat oil in medium frying pan; cook bacon, celery, onion, carrot, and chili, stirring, until onion softens. Add paste; cook, stirring, 1 minute. Transfer mixture to 4½-quart slow cooker. Stir in sauce, stock, sugar, and beans. Cook, covered, on low, 8 hours.
2 Stir in parsley; season to taste.

prep + cook time 8 hours 30 minutes
nutritional count per serving
12.9g total fat (3.9g saturated fat); 266 cal; 17.8g carbohydrate; 17.3g protein; 5.2g fiber

tips Instead of the cannellini beans, you can use any canned white beans you like, such as great northern, navy, or haricot. Use a plain (unflavored) tomato-based sauce suitable for serving over pasta. These sauces can be bought in cans and jars and are often labeled "sugo" or "passata".

❄ suitable to freeze at the end of step 1.

serving suggestion Serve with toasted sourdough or cornbread.

chorizo, chili, and bean stew

serves 6

1 tablespoon olive oil
1 large red onion, chopped coarsely
3 chorizo sausages, chopped coarsely
4 cloves garlic, crushed
1 teaspoon dried chili flakes
1 medium red bell pepper,
  chopped coarsely
5 ounces baby green beans, halved
2 x 15-ounce cans cannellini beans,
  rinsed, drained
28-ounce can diced tomatoes
⅓ cup chicken stock
2 dried bay leaves
⅓ cup coarsely chopped fresh
  flat-leaf parsley

1 Heat oil in large frying pan; cook onion and chorizo, stirring, until browned lightly. Add garlic and chili flakes; cook, stirring, until fragrant.
2 Combine peppers, both beans, undrained tomatoes, stock, bay leaves, and chorizo mixture in 4½-quart slow cooker. Cook, covered, on low, 3 hours.
3 Discard bay leaves. Season to taste; sprinkle with parsley.

prep + cook time 3 hours 20 minutes
nutritional count per serving
28.7g total fat (9.6g saturated fat); 404 cal; 13.1g carbohydrate; 21.3g protein; 5.8g fiber

 suitable to freeze at the end of step 2.

serving suggestion Serve stew with a green salad and some crusty bread.

tomato tripe stew with pancetta

serves 6

3¼ pounds honeycomb tripe
1 tablespoon olive oil
1 medium brown onion, chopped coarsely
2 cloves garlic, crushed
6 slices pancetta (3 ounces),
  chopped coarsely
⅓ cup dry white wine
1 large carrot, chopped coarsely
1 stalk celery, trimmed, chopped coarsely
3 cups bottled tomato pasta sauce
2 dried bay leaves
½ cup coarsely chopped fresh
  flat-leaf parsley

1 Cover tripe with cold water in large saucepan; bring to a boil. Boil, covered, 10 minutes. Drain. Cut tripe into 1½ inch pieces, transfer to 4½-quart slow cooker.
2 Meanwhile, heat oil in small frying pan; cook onion, garlic, and pancetta, stirring, until onion softens and pancetta is browned and crisp.

3 Transfer onion mixture to cooker; stir in wine, carrot, celery, sauce, and bay leaves. Cook, covered, on low, 6 hours.
4 Discard bay leaves. Season to taste. Sprinkle stew with parsley.

prep + cook time 6 hours 30 minutes
nutritional count per serving
11.3g total fat (3.6g saturated fat); 328 cal; 14g carbohydrate; 38.3g protein; 3.9g fiber

tips Check with the butcher to make sure the tripe has been cleaned and blanched. We suggest you blanch the tripe again—see step 1—before cutting it into pieces. You might have to order the tripe from the butcher in advance.
Use a plain (unflavored) tomato-based sauce suitable for serving over pasta. These sauces can be bought in cans and jars and are often labeled "sugo" or "passata".

❄ not suitable to freeze.

serving suggestion Serve stew with crusty bread.

lamb tagine with harissa and green olives   serves 6

2½ pounds boned lamb shoulder, chopped coarsely
1 large red onion, grated coarsely
2 cloves garlic, crushed
2 tablespoons finely chopped coriander (cilantro) root and stem mixture
1 cinnamon stick, halved
1 teaspoon ground cumin
1 teaspoon ground ginger
1 teaspoon sweet paprika
⅓ cup olive oil
1 tablespoon harissa
28-ounce can diced tomatoes
¼ cup tomato paste
½ cup beef stock
15-ounce can chickpeas, rinsed, drained
2 tablespoons honey
½ cup pitted small green olives
2 teaspoons finely chopped preserved lemon rind
½ cup loosely packed fresh mint leaves

1 Combine lamb, onion, garlic, coriander root and stem mixture, spices, and half the oil in large bowl.
2 Heat remaining oil in large frying pan; cook lamb, in batches, until browned all over. Transfer lamb to 4½-quart slow cooker.
3 Stir harissa, undrained tomatoes, paste, stock, chickpeas, and honey into cooker. Cook, covered, on low, 4 hours.
4 Remove cinnamon stick; stir in olives and lemon rind. Season to taste; sprinkle with mint.

prep + cook time 4 hours 35 minutes
nutritional count per serving
32g total fat (10.2g saturated fat); 580 cal; 26.3g carbohydrate; 44.1g protein; 5.7g fiber

tips The lamb mixture can be marinated overnight at the end of step 1. Preserved lemon is available at delis and some supermarkets. Remove and discard the flesh, wash the rind, then use it as the recipe directs.

 suitable to freeze at the end of step 3.

serving suggestion Serve with couscous flavored with chopped preserved lemon rind and coarsely chopped fresh mint leaves.

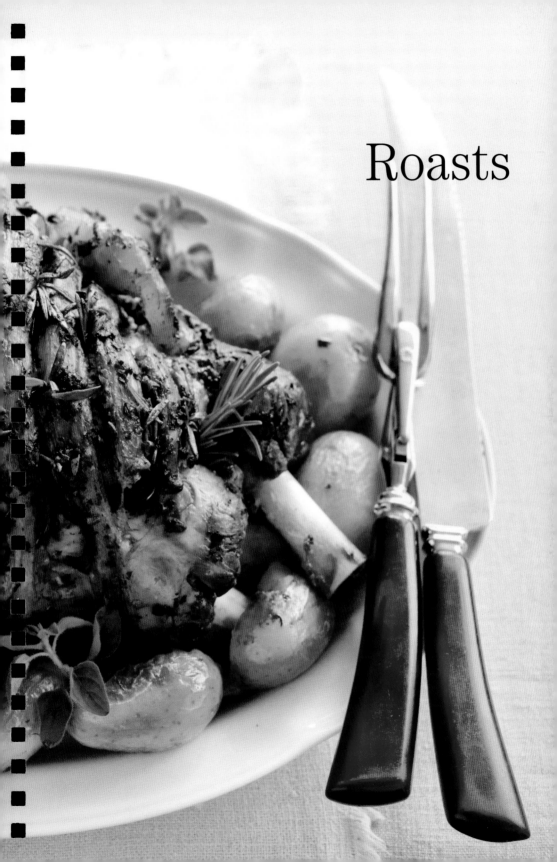

Roasts

chicken with leeks and artichokes

3¼-pound whole chicken
1 unpeeled lemon, chopped coarsely
4 cloves unpeeled garlic
4 sprigs fresh tarragon
6 sprigs fresh flat-leaf parsley
1½ ounces butter
¾ cup dry white wine
2 medium globe artichokes, quartered
8 baby leeks
1 cup chicken stock

serving suggestion Serve chicken with creamy mashed potatoes and a green leafy salad.

1   Wash chicken under cold water; pat dry inside and out with paper towels. Place lemon, garlic, and herbs in chicken cavity; season with salt and pepper. Tuck wing tips under; tie legs together with kitchen string.
2   Melt butter in large frying pan; cook chicken until browned all over. Remove chicken. Add wine; bring to a boil.
3   Meanwhile, trim stems from artichokes; remove tough outer leaves. Place artichokes and leeks in 4½-quart slow cooker; add wine mixture and stock. Place chicken on vegetables; cook, covered, on low, 6 hours.
4   Serve chicken with vegetables; drizzle with a little of the juice.

prep + cook time 6 hours 30 minutes
nutritional count per serving
42.2g total fat (16.3g saturated fat); 615 cal; 5.6g carbohydrate; 44.9g protein; 4.2g fiber

tip Replace the baby leeks with 1 large leek, sliced thickly.

❄ not suitable to freeze.

green olive and lemon chicken

serves 4

1 tablespoon butter, softened
1 tablespoon olive oil
2 teaspoons finely grated lemon rind
3 cloves garlic, crushed
¼ cup pitted green olives, chopped finely
2 tablespoons finely chopped fresh flat-leaf
  parsley
3¼-pound whole chicken
2 unpeeled medium lemons, quartered

1 Combine butter, oil, rind, garlic, olives, and parsley in medium bowl; season.
2 Rinse chicken under cold water; pat dry, inside and out, with paper towels. Use fingers to make a pocket between the breasts and skin; push half the butter mixture under skin. Rub remaining butter mixture all over chicken. Tuck wing tips under; fill cavity with lemon, tie legs together with kitchen string. Trim skin around neck; secure neck flap to underside of chicken with small fine skewers.

3 Place chicken in 4½-quart slow cooker. Cook, covered, on low, 6 hours.
4 Cut chicken into quarters to serve.

prep + cook time 6 hours 20 minutes
nutritional count per serving
38.1g total fat (12.1g saturated fat); 499 cal; 2g carbohydrate; 37.7g protein; 0.6g fiber

tip Kitchen string is made of a natural product such as cotton or hemp so that it doesn't affect the flavor of the food it's tied around nor melts when heated.

❄ not suitable to freeze.

serving suggestion Serve with roasted potatoes and steamed green vegetables, or creamy polenta or mashed potatoes and a green salad.

pork neck with cider and pear

serves 4

2-pound piece pork neck
6 ounces Italian pork sausages
1 egg yolk
½ cup coarsely chopped pistachios
2 tablespoons coarsely chopped fresh sage
1 tablespoon olive oil
1 medium brown onion, quartered
4 cloves garlic, halved
2 medium unpeeled pears, quartered
⅔ cup hard apple cider
6 fresh sage leaves

1 Place pork on cutting board; slice through thickest part of pork horizontally, without cutting all the way through. Open pork out to form one large piece; trim pork.
2 Squeeze filling from sausages into small bowl, mix in egg yolk, nuts, and chopped sage; season. Press sausage mixture along one long side of pork; roll pork to enclose filling. Tie pork with kitchen string at 1-inch intervals.

serving suggestion Serve pork with creamy mashed potatoes and a radicchio or endive salad.

3 Heat oil in large frying pan; cook pork until browned all over. Remove from pan. Add onion and garlic to same pan; cook, stirring, until onion softens.
4 Place pears and onion mixture in 4½-quart slow cooker; top with pork then add cider and sage leaves. Cook, covered, on low, 6 hours.
5 Serve sliced pork with pear and onion mixture. Sprinkle with extra sage leaves, if you like.

prep + cook time 6 hours 30 minutes
nutritional count per serving
45.3g total fat (13g saturated fat); 757 cal; 19g carbohydrate; 63g protein; 5.6g fiber

tip Italian sausages are coarse pork sausages generally sold in plump links. They are usually flavored with garlic and fennel seed or anise seed, and come in two styles—hot (flavored with red chili) and sweet (without the added heat). They are available from butchers, delicatessens, and some supermarkets.

❄ not suitable to freeze.

beef pot roast

¼ cup olive oil
4 small potatoes, unpeeled, halved
12-ounce piece unpeeled pumpkin,
　cut into 4 wedges
8 baby onions, halved
12 ounces baby carrots
8 ounces Jerusalem artichokes
　(sunchokes)
1½-pound piece beef blade steak
1 tablespoon whole grain mustard
2 teaspoons smoked paprika
2 teaspoons finely chopped fresh rosemary
1 clove garlic, crushed
1½ cups beef stock
½ cup dry red wine
2 tablespoons balsamic vinegar
¼ cup powdered gravy mix
2 tablespoons water

1 Heat 2 tablespoons of the oil in large frying pan; cook potato, pumpkin, and onion, in batches, until browned all over. Place vegetables in 4½-quart slow cooker with carrots and artichokes.
2 Heat 2 teaspoons of the remaining oil in same pan; cook beef until browned all over. Remove beef from pan; spread with combined mustard, paprika, rosemary, garlic, and remaining oil.
3 Place beef on vegetables in slow cooker; pour over combined stock, wine, and vinegar. Cook, covered, on low, 8 hours.
4 Remove beef and vegetables from cooker; cover beef, stand 10 minutes before slicing thinly. Cover vegetables to keep warm.
5 Meanwhile, blend gravy powder with the water in small bowl until smooth. Stir gravy mixture into liquid in slow cooker; cook, covered, on high, about 10 minutes or until gravy is thickened slightly. Season to taste. Strain gravy.
6 Serve beef with gravy and vegetables.

prep + cook time 8 hours 30 minutes
nutritional count per serving
26.8g total fat (7.5g saturated fat); 563 cal; 25g carbohydrate; 46.8g protein; 7.1g fiber

serving suggestion Serve with steamed green beans or broccoli.

tips Jerusalem artichokes can be hard to find. You can leave them out and add rutabaga, parsnip, or turnip to the pot roast instead.
Gravy powder is an instant gravy mix made with browned flour. All-purpose flour can be used for thickening instead.

❄ not suitable to freeze.

mexican slow-roasted lamb shanks serves 4

2 medium tomatoes, chopped coarsely
1 medium red bell pepper, chopped coarsely
1 medium yellow bell pepper,
  chopped coarsely
2 tablespoons olive oil
2 teaspoons sweet paprika
2 teaspoons ground cumin
1 teaspoon ground coriander
2 cloves garlic, crushed
1 fresh long red chili, chopped finely
2 tablespoons finely chopped fresh oregano
8 French-trimmed lamb shanks (4¼ pounds)

1 Combine tomato and peppers in 4½-quart slow cooker.
2 Combine oil, spices, garlic, chili, and oregano in large bowl; add lamb, turn to coat in marinade. Cook lamb in heated large frying pan, in batches, until browned. Transfer to cooker. Cook, covered, on low, 8 hours. Season to taste.
3 Serve lamb shanks drizzled with sauce; sprinkle with extra oregano leaves.

prep + cook time 8 hours 30 minutes
nutritional count per serving
14.1g total fat (3.5g saturated fat); 397 cal; 4.2g carbohydrate; 61.9g protein; 2g fiber

tip Lamb can be marinated in the spice mixture overnight, if you like.

❄ suitable to freeze at the end of step 2.

serving suggestion Serve lamb with flour tortillas, lime wedges, and a green salad.

portuguese-style chicken

¼ cup olive oil
¼ cup tomato paste
4 cloves garlic, quartered
2 tablespoons finely grated lemon rind
⅓ cup lemon juice
4 fresh small red Thai (serrano) chilies,
  chopped coarsely
1 tablespoon smoked paprika
½ cup firmly packed fresh oregano leaves
3¾-pound whole chicken
1 medium unpeeled lemon, quartered
3 sprigs fresh lemon thyme

1 Blend or process 2 tablespoons of the oil, paste, garlic, rind, juice, chili, paprika, and oregano until smooth. Season to taste.
2 Rinse chicken under cold water; pat dry inside and out with paper towels. Place lemon quarters and thyme inside cavity of chicken; secure cavity with a fine skewer.

3 Make a pocket under skin of breast, drumsticks and thighs with fingers. Using disposable gloves, rub ¼ cup of paste under skin. Tuck wing tips under; tie legs together with kitchen string. Rub ¼ cup of paste all over chicken.
4 Heat remaining oil in large frying pan; cook chicken until browned all over. Transfer to 4½-quart slow cooker. Cook, covered, on low, 6 hours.
5 Cut chicken into pieces; accompany with the remaining paste.

prep + cook time 6 hours 45 minutes
nutritional count per serving
50g total fat (13.2g saturated fat); 643 cal; 2.9g carbohydrate; 45.8g protein; 1.5g fiber

tip Fresh chilies can burn your fingers so wear disposable gloves when handling them.

❄ not suitable to freeze.

serving suggestion Serve chicken with French fries or potato wedges, a green salad, and lemon wedges.

slow-roasted chili and fennel pork

serves 6

2-pound piece pork shoulder on the bone, rind on
1 medium lemon
1½ tablespoons fennel seeds
2 teaspoons dried chili flakes
2 teaspoons sea salt
½ teaspoon cracked black pepper
3 cloves garlic, chopped coarsely
⅓ cup olive oil
1 large brown onion, chopped coarsely
½ cup chicken stock

1 Using a sharp knife, score pork rind in a criss-cross pattern. Coarsely grate rind from lemon; chop lemon coarsely.
2 Cook fennel seeds in dry large frying pan until fragrant. Using mortar and pestle, crush seeds. Add chili, salt, pepper, garlic, lemon rind, and 2 tablespoons of the oil; pound until ground finely.
3 Heat remaining oil in same pan; cook pork, skin-side down, until browned and crisp. Turn pork; cook until browned all over. Spread fennel mixture all over pork. Place onion, stock, and chopped lemon in 4½-quart slow cooker; top with pork, skin-side up. Cook, covered, on low, 7 hours.
4 Remove pork from cooker; stand, covered, 10 minutes before slicing thinly.

prep + cook time 7 hours 30 minutes
nutritional count per serving
24.3g total fat (6.4g saturated fat); 331 cal; 2.1g carbohydrate; 26.1g protein; 0.7g fiber

tip Ask the butcher to score the rind on the pork for you.

❄ not suitable to freeze.

serving suggestion Serve sliced pork with your favorite chutney or relish in crusty bread rolls or baguettes with a green salad.

char siu pork ribs

serves 6

5¼ pounds pork spare ribs
2 tablespoons peanut oil
½ cup char siu sauce
2 tablespoons light soy sauce
¼ cup orange juice
2-inch piece fresh ginger, grated
2 cloves garlic, crushed
1 fresh long red chili, chopped finely
2 teaspoons sesame oil

1 Cut rib racks into pieces to fit 4½-quart slow cooker. Heat peanut oil in large frying pan; cook ribs, in batches, until browned all over.
2 Meanwhile, combine sauces, juice, ginger, garlic, chili, and sesame oil in bowl; brush all over ribs. Place ribs in cooker; pour over remaining sauce. Cook, covered, on low, 7 hours.

3 Remove ribs from sauce; cover to keep warm. Place sauce in medium saucepan; bring to a boil. Boil, uncovered, about 5 minutes or until sauce is thickened slightly.
4 Serve ribs drizzled with sauce.

prep + cook time 7 hours 25 minutes
nutritional count per serving
23.9g total fat (6.6g saturated fat); 421 cal; 9.6g carbohydrate; 40.7g protein; 2.7g fiber

tip Ask the butcher to cut the rib racks into pieces that will fit your slow cooker.

❄ not suitable to freeze.

serving suggestion Serve ribs with steamed rice and stir-fried Asian greens.

greek-style roast lamb with potatoes

serves 4

2 tablespoons olive oil
2 pounds baby new potatoes
4-pound lamb leg
2 sprigs fresh rosemary, chopped coarsely
2 tablespoons finely chopped fresh
   flat-leaf parsley
2 tablespoons finely chopped fresh oregano
3 cloves garlic, crushed
1 tablespoon finely grated lemon rind
2 tablespoons lemon juice
½ cup beef stock

1 Heat half the oil in large frying pan;
cook potatoes until browned. Transfer to
4½-quart slow cooker.
2 Make small cuts in lamb at 1-inch
intervals; press rosemary into cuts.
Combine remaining oil, parsley, oregano,
garlic, rind, and juice in small bowl; rub
mixture all over lamb, season.

3 Cook lamb in same heated pan until
browned all over. Place lamb on top of
potatoes; add stock. Cook, covered, on
low, 8 hours.
4 Remove lamb and potatoes; cover lamb,
stand 10 minutes before slicing.
5 Serve lamb with potatoes and sauce.

prep + cook time 8 hours 40 minutes
nutritional count per serving
29.5g total fat (10.2g saturated fat); 767 cal;
33.5g carbohydrate; 88.4g protein; 5.6g fiber

❄ not suitable to freeze. Lamb can be
covered and refrigerated overnight at step 2.

serving suggestion Serve lamb with a Greek
salad or steamed spinach.

lamb with quince and honey

2-pound piece boneless lamb shoulder
6 cloves garlic, peeled, halved
2 tablespoons finely chopped coriander
(cilantro) root and stem mixture
2 teaspoons ground cumin
1 teaspoon ground coriander
1 teaspoon sweet paprika
2 tablespoons olive oil
1 medium brown onion, sliced thickly
1 cup chicken stock
1 cinnamon stick
2 tablespoons honey
1/3 cup coarsely chopped fresh coriander
(cilantro) leaves
1 tablespoon quince paste

1 Roll and tie lamb with kitchen string at 2-inch intervals. Using mortar and pestle, crush garlic, coriander root and stem mixture, spices, and half the oil until almost smooth. Rub garlic mixture all over lamb; cover, refrigerate 2 hours.

2 Heat remaining oil in large frying pan; cook lamb, until browned all over. Remove from pan. Add onion to same pan; cook, stirring, until onion softens.

3 Place stock, cinnamon, and onion mixture in 4½-quart slow cooker; top with lamb, drizzle with honey. Season with salt and pepper. Cook, covered, on low, 8 hours. Stand lamb 10 minutes; stir quince paste into sauce.

4 Thickly slice lamb, serve with sauce; sprinkle with chopped coriander.

prep + cook time 8 hours 25 minutes
(+ refrigeration)
nutritional count per serving
31.5g total fat (11.4g saturated fat); 566 cal; 15.8g carbohydrate; 54g protein; 1.9g fiber

tip Cover and refrigerate lamb overnight at the end of step 1, if you like.

❅ not suitable to freeze.

serving suggestion Serve lamb with couscous.

Curries

red curry lamb shanks

serves 6

2 tablespoons vegetable oil
6 French-trimmed lamb shanks (4¼ pounds)
1 large sweet potato, chopped coarsely
3 fresh kaffir lime leaves, shredded thinly
1 large brown onion, chopped finely
2 tablespoons red curry paste
1⅔ cups canned coconut cream
2 cups chicken stock
2 tablespoons fish sauce
12 ounces snake beans, chopped coarsely
1 cup loosely packed fresh coriander
   (cilantro) leaves
2 tablespoons lime juice

serving suggestion Serve curry with
steamed rice.

1   Heat half the oil in large frying pan; cook
lamb, in batches, until browned all over.
Place lamb in 4½-quart slow cooker, add
sweet potato and lime leaves.
2   Heat remaining oil in same pan; cook
onion, stirring, until soft. Add curry paste;
cook, stirring, until fragrant. Add coconut
cream; bring to a boil. Remove pan from
heat; stir in stock and sauce, pour over
lamb. Cook, covered, on low, 8 hours.
3   Add beans to cooker; cook, covered, on
high, about 15 minutes. Stir in coriander
and juice; season to taste.

prep + cook time 8 hours 40 minutes
nutritional count per serving
33.2g total fat (18g saturated fat); 559 cal;
17g carbohydrate; 45.6g protein; 6g fiber

tips If you can't find snake beans, use
regular green beans instead.
Red curry paste is available in various
strengths from supermarkets. Use
whichever one suits your spice-level
tolerance best.

❄ suitable to freeze at the end of step 2.

lemon grass pork curry

serves 6

2 x 4-inch sticks fresh lemon grass,
  chopped coarsely
3 cloves garlic, quartered
1½-inch piece fresh galangal,
  sliced thinly
1 fresh small red Thai (serrano) chili,
  chopped coarsely
1 teaspoon ground turmeric
½ teaspoon ground cumin
¼ teaspoon ground cardamom
3 fresh kaffir lime leaves, shredded thinly
1 medium red onion, chopped coarsely
½ cup water
1 tablespoon peanut oil
2½ pounds pork neck, chopped coarsely
3⅓ cups canned coconut milk
3 baby eggplants, sliced thickly
12 ounces baby carrots, halved lengthwise
1 tablespoon fish sauce
2 tablespoons lime juice
½ cup loosely packed fresh coriander
  (cilantro) leaves

1 Blend or process lemon grass, garlic,
galangal, chili, spices, lime leaves, onion,
and the water until mixture is smooth.
2 Heat oil in medium frying pan; cook
lemon grass paste, stirring, about 5 minutes
or until fragrant.
3 Transfer lemon grass mixture to
4½-quart slow cooker; stir in pork, coconut
milk, and eggplant. Cook, covered, on low,
4 hours.
4 Add carrots; cook, covered, on low,
2 hours. Stir in sauce and juice; season to
taste. Sprinkle curry with coriander.

prep + cook time 6 hours 30 minutes
nutritional count per serving
46.9g total fat (30.2g saturated fat); 660 cal;
10.9g carbohydrate; 46.6g protein; 5.8g fiber

❋ not suitable to freeze.

serving suggestion Serve curry with
steamed rice.

tamarind and coconut pork curry

1 tablespoon peanut oil
2½ pounds boned pork shoulder,
  chopped coarsely
1 medium brown onion, chopped finely
2 cloves garlic, crushed
1 fresh long red chili, sliced thinly
1½-inch piece fresh ginger, grated
2 teaspoons fenugreek seeds
1 teaspoon ground cumin
1 teaspoon ground ginger
½ teaspoon ground cinnamon
½ teaspoon ground cardamom
8 fresh curry leaves
1 tablespoon tamarind concentrate
1¼ cups canned coconut cream
1 cup chicken stock
6 ounces green beans, halved
1 cup toasted shredded coconut

serving suggestion Serve curry with
steamed rice.

1 Heat oil in large frying pan; cook pork, in
batches, until browned. Remove from pan.
2 Cook onion, garlic, chili, and ginger in
same heated pan, stirring, until onion
softens. Add spices and curry leaves; cook,
stirring, until fragrant.
3 Transfer onion mixture to 4½-quart slow
cooker; stir in pork, tamarind, coconut
cream, and stock. Cook, covered, on low,
6 hours.
4 Add beans and half the coconut; cook,
covered, on high 20 minutes or until beans
are tender. Season to taste; sprinkle curry
with remaining coconut.

prep + cook time 6 hours 40 minutes
nutritional count per serving
36.8g total fat (21.4g saturated fat); 539 cal;
5.2g carbohydrate; 45.6g protein; 4.1g fiber

❄ not suitable to freeze.

chicken, lentil, and pumpkin curry

serves 6

⅔ cup dried brown lentils
⅔ cup dried red lentils
1 tablespoon vegetable oil
1 large brown onion, chopped finely
2 cloves garlic, crushed
1-inch piece fresh ginger, grated
2 teaspoons ground cumin
2 teaspoons ground coriander
2 teaspoons black mustard seeds
1 teaspoon ground turmeric
1 fresh long red chili, chopped finely
3 cups chicken stock
2 pounds chicken thigh filets,
  chopped coarsely
14½-ounce can diced tomatoes
1 pound pumpkin, chopped coarsely
1¼ cups canned coconut milk
5 ounces baby spinach leaves
½ cup coarsely chopped fresh coriander
  (cilantro)

1 Rinse lentils under cold water until water runs clear; drain. Heat oil in large frying pan; cook onion, garlic, and ginger, stirring, until onion softens. Add spices and chili; cook, stirring, until fragrant. Add stock; bring to a boil.

2 Pour stock mixture into 4½-quart slow cooker; stir in chicken, undrained tomatoes, pumpkin, and lentils. Cook, covered, on low, 7 hours.

3 Stir in coconut milk; cook, covered, on high, 15 minutes, stirring once. Stir in spinach and coriander. Season to taste.

prep + cook time 7 hours 40 minutes
nutritional count per serving
26.3g total fat (12.8g saturated fat); 553 cal; 27.6g carbohydrate; 47g protein; 10g fiber

❄ suitable to freeze at the end of step 2.

serving suggestion Serve curry with chapatis and plain yogurt.

creamy vegetable and almond korma

serves 6

½ cup korma paste
½ cup ground almonds
1 large brown onion, sliced thinly
2 cloves garlic, crushed
½ cup vegetable stock
½ cup water
1⅓ cups light cream
12 ounces baby carrots
4 ounces baby corn
1 pound baby potatoes, halved
12 ounces pumpkin, chopped coarsely
10 ounces cauliflower, cut into florets
6 medium yellow patty-pan squash, halved
½ cup frozen peas
½ cup roasted slivered almonds
2 teaspoons black sesame seeds

serving suggestion Serve korma with steamed rice, naan, and yogurt.

1 Combine paste, ground almonds, onion, garlic, stock, the water, cream, carrots, corn, potato, pumpkin, and cauliflower in 4½-quart slow cooker. Cook, covered, on low, 6 hours.
2 Add squash and peas; cook, covered, on high, about 20 minutes. Season to taste. Sprinkle curry with nuts and seeds.

prep + cook time 6 hours 45 minutes
nutritional count per serving
42.8g total fat (16.2g saturated fat); 581 cal; 29.6g carbohydrate; 14.4g protein; 12.4g fiber

tip This is a mild curry. For more heat, serve curry sprinkled with some sliced fresh red chili.

❄ suitable to freeze at the end of step 1.

lamb rogan josh

3¼ pounds boned lamb shoulder,
    chopped coarsely
2 large brown onions, sliced thinly
2-inch piece fresh ginger, grated
3 cloves garlic, crushed
½ cup rogan josh paste
2 tablespoons tomato paste
14½-ounce canned diced tomatoes
½ cup beef stock
1 cinnamon stick
4 cardamom pods, bruised
2 dried bay leaves
½ cup loosely packed fresh coriander
    (cilantro) leaves

1 Combine lamb, onion, ginger, garlic, pastes, undrained tomatoes, stock, cinnamon, cardamom, and bay leaves in 4½-quart slow cooker. Cook, covered, on low, 8 hours. Season to taste.

2 Sprinkle curry with coriander.

prep + cook time 8 hours 20 minutes
nutritional count per serving
30.1g total fat (10.8g saturated fat); 538 cal; 8.8g carbohydrate; 55.7g protein; 5.1g fiber

❄ suitable to freeze at the end of step 1.

serving suggestion Serve lamb with steamed rice, naan, and yogurt.

indian vegetable curry

1 tablespoon vegetable oil
1 medium leek, sliced thickly
2 cloves garlic, crushed
2 teaspoons black mustard seeds
2 teaspoons ground cumin
2 teaspoons garam masala
1 teaspoon ground turmeric
1½ cups vegetable stock
14½-ounce can diced tomatoes
1 large sweet potato, chopped coarsely
1 large carrot, chopped coarsely
1⅔ cups canned coconut milk
12 ounces brussels sprouts, halved
15-ounce can chickpeas, rinsed, drained
5 ounces baby spinach leaves
½ cup coarsely chopped fresh coriander
  (cilantro)

1 Heat oil in large frying pan; cook leek and garlic, stirring, until leek softens. Add spices; cook, stirring, until fragrant. Add stock; bring to a boil.
2 Pour stock mixture into 4½-quart slow cooker; stir in undrained tomatoes, sweet potato, carrot, and coconut milk. Cook, covered, on low, 4 hours.
3 Add sprouts and chickpeas to curry. Cook, covered, on high, about 40 minutes or until sprouts are just tender.
4 Stir in spinach and coriander. Season to taste.

prep + cook time 5 hours
nutritional count per serving
18.7g total fat (12.8g saturated fat); 332 cal; 25.4g carbohydrate; 10.7g protein; 10.6g fiber

❄ suitable to freeze at the end of step 3.

serving suggestion Serve curry with naan bread and lemon wedges.

butter chicken

12 chicken thigh cutlets (5¼ pounds),
  skin removed
2 tablespoons lemon juice
1 teaspoon chili powder
¾ cup Greek-style yogurt
2-inch piece fresh ginger, grated
2 teaspoons garam masala
1½ ounces butter
1 tablespoon vegetable oil
1 medium brown onion, chopped finely
4 cloves garlic, crushed
1 teaspoon ground coriander
1 teaspoon ground cumin
1 teaspoon sweet paprika
2 tablespoons tomato paste
1⅔ cups canned tomato puree
⅔ cup chicken stock
2 tablespoons honey
1 cinnamon stick
⅓ cup light cream
⅓ cup ricotta cheese
½ cup loosely packed fresh coriander
  (cilantro) leaves

1 Combine chicken, juice, and chili powder in large bowl. Cover, refrigerate 30 minutes.
2 Stir yogurt, ginger, and half the garam masala into chicken mixture.
3 Heat butter and oil in large frying pan; cook chicken, in batches, until browned all over. Transfer chicken to 4½-quart slow cooker. Add onion and garlic to same pan; cook, stirring, until onion softens. Add remaining garam masala and ground spices; cook, stirring, until fragrant. Remove from heat; stir in tomato paste, puree, stock, honey, and cinnamon. Transfer tomato mixture to slow cooker. Cook, covered, on low, 4 hours.
4 Stir in cream; season to taste.
5 Serve topped with ricotta and coriander leaves.

prep + cook time 4 hours 30 minutes (+ refrigeration)
nutritional count per serving
39.3g total fat (17g saturated fat); 658 cal; 17.9g carbohydrate; 57.8g protein; 2.6g fiber

 suitable to freeze at the end of step 3.

serving suggestion Serve chicken with steamed basmati rice and warm naan bread.

old-fashioned curried sausages

serves 6

12 thick beef sausages (4 pounds)
1 tablespoon vegetable oil
2 medium brown onions, sliced thinly
2 tablespoons mild curry powder
14½-ounce can diced tomatoes
1 cup beef stock
1 cup water
4 medium potatoes, unpeeled, cut into
  thick wedges
1 cup frozen peas, thawed
½ cup golden raisins

1 Place sausages in large saucepan, add enough cold water to cover sausages; bring to a boil. Boil, uncovered, 2 minutes; drain.

2 Heat oil in same pan; cook onion, stirring, until softened. Add curry powder; cook, stirring, until fragrant. Remove from heat; stir in undrained tomatoes, stock, and the water.

3 Place potatoes in 4½-quart slow cooker; top with sausages and onion mixture. Cook, covered, on low, 8 hours.

4 Stir in peas and raisins. Season to taste.

prep + cook time 8 hours 20 minutes
nutritional count per serving
79.8g total fat (37g saturated fat); 1061 cal; 40g carbohydrate; 41.3g protein; 13.7g fiber

❄ not suitable to freeze.

serving suggestion Serve with crusty bread.

spinach dhal

1 pound yellow split peas
3 tablespoons ghee
2 medium brown onions, chopped finely
3 cloves garlic, crushed
1½-inch piece fresh ginger, grated
1 fresh long green chili, chopped finely
2 tablespoons black mustard seeds
1 teaspoon cumin seeds
1 tablespoon ground coriander
2 teaspoons ground turmeric
1 teaspoon garam masala
28-ounce can diced tomatoes
3 cups vegetable stock
1½ cups water
1 teaspoon superfine sugar
4 medium swiss chard leaves (11 ounces),
  stems removed, chopped coarsely

1 Rinse split peas under cold water until water runs clear; drain.
2 Heat ghee in large frying pan; cook onion, garlic, ginger, and chili, stirring, until onion softens. Add seeds and spices; cook, stirring, until fragrant. Place onion mixture into 4½-quart slow cooker; stir in undrained tomatoes, stock, the water, sugar, and peas. Cook, covered, on low, 10 hours.
3 Stir in swiss chard; season to taste.

prep + cook time 10 hours 20 minutes
nutritional count per serving
10.1g total fat (5.4g saturated fat); 404 cal; 48.2g carbohydrate; 23.3g protein; 12.5g fiber

❄ suitable to freeze at the end of step 2.

serving suggestion Serve dhal topped with fried or caramelized onions.

spiced chicken in coconut sauce

serves 6

1 tablespoon peanut oil
3 chicken thigh filets, halved
6 chicken drumsticks
2 medium brown onions, chopped coarsely
1 cup chicken stock
1⅔ cups canned coconut milk
3 fresh kaffir lime leaves, shredded thinly
10 ounces green beans, chopped coarsely
12 fresh Thai eggplants, halved
¾ cup loosely packed fresh coriander
   (cilantro) leaves

SPICE PASTE
4 shallots, quartered
2 cloves garlic, chopped coarsely
2-inch piece fresh ginger,
   chopped coarsely
2 teaspoons ground cumin
2 teaspoons ground coriander
2 teaspoons ground turmeric
3 fresh small red Thai (serrano) chilies,
   chopped coarsely
2 tablespoons fish sauce
2 tablespoons peanut oil
2 tablespoons lime juice
1 tablespoon grated palm sugar

1 Make spice paste.
2 Heat half the oil in large frying pan; cook chicken, in batches, until browned all over, place in 4½-quart slow cooker. Heat remaining oil in same pan; cook onion, stirring, until soft. Add spice paste; cook, stirring, until fragrant. Add stock; bring to a boil.
3 Remove from heat; stir in coconut milk and lime leaves, pour over chicken. Cook, covered, on low, 7 hours.
4 Add beans and eggplant, cook, covered, on high, about 20 minutes or until vegetables are tender. Season to taste; sprinkle with coriander.
spice paste Blend or process ingredients until mixture is smooth.

prep + cook time 7 hours 45 minutes
nutritional count per serving
41.9g total fat (19.4g saturated fat); 600 cal;
11.6g carbohydrate; 42.5g protein; 5.5g fiber

❄ suitable to freeze at the end of step 3.

serving suggestion Serve chicken with steamed rice and lime wedges.

duck vindaloo

3¾-pound whole duck
¼ cup all-purpose flour
1 tablespoon peanut oil
2 teaspoons cumin seeds
2 teaspoons fenugreek seeds
1 teaspoon ground coriander
1 teaspoon ground turmeric
½ teaspoon ground cardamom
4 fresh small red Thai (serrano) chilies,
  chopped coarsely
3 cloves garlic, quartered
1-inch piece fresh ginger, sliced thinly
⅓ cup white vinegar
½ cup chicken stock
1 medium red onion, chopped finely
4 medium potatoes, chopped coarsely
2 tablespoons powdered chicken gravy mix
2 tablespoons water
½ cup loosely packed fresh coriander
  (cilantro) leaves

1 Rinse duck under cold water; pat dry. Cut duck into six serving-sized pieces. Toss duck in flour, shake off excess. Heat oil in large frying pan; cook duck, in batches, until browned. Transfer to 4½-quart slow cooker.

2 Meanwhile, dry-fry spices in small frying pan until fragrant; cool. Blend or process spices, chili, garlic, ginger, and vinegar until smooth.

3 Stir spice mixture into cooker with stock, onion, and potato. Cook, covered, on low, 6 hours. Season to taste.

4 Transfer duck and potato to serving plate. Skim excess fat from sauce. Stir combined gravy powder and the water into sauce in slow cooker. Cook, covered, on high, about 10 minutes or until the sauce thickens.

5 Drizzle sauce over duck; sprinkle with coriander.

prep + cook time 6 hours 45 minutes
nutritional count per serving
66.5g total fat (19.6g saturated fat); 795 cal; 22.7g carbohydrate; 26.7g protein; 3g fiber

tip This is a mild vindaloo. If you like it hotter, add more fresh chilies when you make the paste.

❄ not suitable to freeze.

serving suggestion Serve vindaloo with steamed rice.

Accompaniments

soft polenta Combine 3 cups water and 2 cups vegetable stock in large saucepan; bring to a boil. Gradually stir in 2 cups polenta. Simmer, stirring, about 10 minutes or until polenta thickens. Add 1 cup milk, 2 tablespoons butter, and ¼ cup finely grated parmesan cheese; stir until cheese melts.

parsnip mash Boil, steam, or microwave 2 pounds chopped parsnip until tender; drain. Mash parsnip in medium bowl with ¾ cup hot milk until smooth; stir in 2 crushed garlic cloves and 2½ tablespoons soft butter. (Note: the same amount of sweet potato, celeriac, or pumpkin can be used instead of parsnip.)

roast potatoes Preheat oven to 375°F. Lightly oil oven tray. Boil, steam or microwave 6 halved medium potatoes for 5 minutes; drain. Pat dry with paper towels; cool 10 minutes. Gently rake rounded sides of potatoes with tines of fork; place potato, in single layer, cut-side down, on oven tray. Brush with 2 tablespoons olive oil; roast, uncovered, in oven, 50 minutes or until browned lightly and crisp.

couscous Combine 1½ cups couscous with 1½ cups boiling water in large heatproof bowl, cover; stand about 5 minutes or until water is absorbed, fluffing with fork occasionally. Stir in 2 ounces finely shredded baby spinach leaves or some coarsely chopped fresh herbs of your choice, or 2 finely chopped green onions (scallions).

creamy mashed potatoes Boil, steam, or microwave 1½ pounds coarsely chopped potatoes until tender; drain. Mash the potatoes with 4 tablespoons soft butter and ½ cup hot cream in medium bowl until smooth.

steamed gai lan in oyster sauce Boil, steam, or microwave 2 pounds halved gai lan until tender; drain. Heat 1 tablespoon peanut oil in wok; stir-fry gai lan, 2 tablespoons oyster sauce and 1 tablespoon light soy sauce about 2 minutes or until mixture is heated through.

pilaf Melt 2 tablespoons butter in medium saucepan; cook 1 crushed garlic clove, stirring, until fragrant. Add 1 cup basmati rice; cook, stirring, 1 minute. Add 1 cup chicken stock and 1 cup water; bring to a boil. Simmer, covered, about 20 minutes or until rice is tender. Remove from heat; fluff rice with fork. Stir in ¼ cup coarsely chopped fresh flat-leaf parsley and ¼ cup roasted sliced almonds.

tomato and herb salad Place 5 coarsely chopped medium tomatoes, 2 tablespoons chopped fresh mint, ¼ cup chopped fresh flat-leaf parsley, and 2 tablespoons chopped fresh dill in medium bowl. Place 2 cloves crushed garlic, 2 tablespoons lemon juice, 1 tablespoon olive oil, and 2 teaspoons white vinegar in screw-top jar; shake well. Drizzle dressing over salad; toss to combine.

Desserts

vanilla and red wine poached pears

serves 6

6 medium firm pears
2 cups dry red wine
1½ cups water
2-inch piece orange rind
½ cup orange juice
1 cup superfine sugar
1 vanilla bean
1 cinnamon stick

serving suggestion Serve with whipped cream or vanilla ice cream.

1 Peel pears, leaving stems intact.
2 Combine wine, the water, rind, juice, and sugar in 4½-quart slow cooker. Halve vanilla bean lengthwise, scrape seeds into slow cooker; add vanilla bean and cinnamon stick.
3 Lay pears down in cooker to cover in wine mixture. Cook, covered, on high, about 4½ hours or until pears are tender. Place 1 cup of the poaching liquid in small saucepan; bring to a boil. Boil, uncovered, about 7 minutes or until syrup is reduced by about half; cool.
4 Meanwhile, place pears in large deep bowl; add remaining poaching liquid, cool.
5 Serve pears drizzled with syrup.

prep + cook time 4 hours 50 minutes (+ cooling)
nutritional count per serving
0.2g total fat (0g saturated fat); 293 cal; 55.9g carbohydrate; 0.8g protein; 3.3g fiber

tips Store leftover poaching liquid in refrigerator for up to 1 month. Use for poaching more pears or stone fruit. We used bartlett pears in this recipe.

❄ not suitable to freeze.

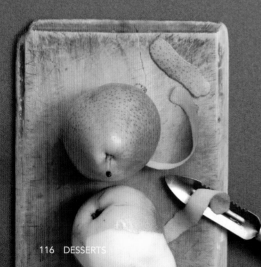

nutty baked apples with butterscotch sauce   serves 6

6 small green apples
6 tablespoons butter, chopped finely
¼ cup slivered almonds
¼ cup finely chopped walnuts
½ teaspoon ground cinnamon
1 cup firmly packed light brown sugar
¾ cup light cream
½ cup apple juice

1   Core unpeeled apples about three-quarters of the way through, making hole 1½ inches in diameter. Use small sharp knife to score around center of each apple.

serving suggestion Serve apples with custard, cream, or ice cream.

2   Combine one-third of the butter with nuts, cinnamon, and ¼ cup of the sugar in small bowl. Press mixture into apple cavities.

3   Combine cream, juice, remaining butter, and sugar in 4½-quart slow cooker. Stand apples upright in sauce. Cook, covered, on high, about 2½ hours, turning apples once, or until apples are tender.

4   Remove apples from cooker; cover to keep warm. Drain sauce into small saucepan; bring to a boil. Boil, uncovered, about 5 minutes or until sauce is thickened slightly.

5   Serve apples drizzled with sauce.

prep + cook time 3 hours 20 minutes
nutritional count per serving
32.1g total fat (17.1g saturated fat); 504 cal; 50.1g carbohydrate; 2.9g protein; 2.8g fiber

tip   Make sure the apples don't touch the side of the slow cooker.

❄ not suitable to freeze.

fig and cranberry bread pudding

serves 6

10 ounces crusty white bread, sliced thickly
½ cup fig jam (conserve)
½ cup finely chopped dried cranberries
2½ cups milk
2⅓ cups light cream
½ cup superfine sugar
1 teaspoon vanilla extract
6 eggs

1 Grease 4½-quart slow cooker bowl. Spread bread slices with jam. Layer bread, overlapping, in cooker bowl; sprinkle with cranberries.

2 Combine milk, cream, sugar, and extract in medium saucepan; bring to a boil. Whisk eggs in medium bowl; gradually whisk in hot milk mixture. Pour custard over bread; stand 5 minutes.

3 Cook, covered, on low, about 4 hours (do not lift the lid during the cooking process, see tip).

4 Remove bowl from cooker. Stand pudding 5 minutes before serving. Serve pudding dusted with a little confectioner's sugar.

prep + cook time 4 hours 20 minutes
nutritional count per serving
54.6g total fat (33.2g saturated fat); 878 cal; 78.8g carbohydrate; 17.2g protein; 2.9g fiber

tips It's important not to lift the lid when cooking the pudding, as the condensation runs down the side of the cooker and causes damp patches on the pudding. We used a small French loaf in this recipe.

❄ not suitable to freeze.

serving suggestion Serve pudding with cream and/or ice cream.

steamed christmas pudding

2½ cups chopped mixed dried fruit
¾ cup finely chopped dried pitted dates
½ cup finely chopped dried cranberries
¾ cup water
1 cup firmly packed dark brown sugar
6 tablespoons butter, chopped coarsely
1 teaspoon baking soda
2 eggs, beaten lightly
¾ cup all-purpose flour
¾ cup self-rising flour
1 teaspoon pie spice
½ teaspoon ground cinnamon
¼ cup dark rum

1   Combine fruit, the water, sugar, and butter in medium saucepan. Stir over heat until butter melts and sugar dissolves; bring to a boil. Reduce heat; simmer, uncovered, 5 minutes. Transfer mixture to large heatproof bowl, stir in baking soda; cool 10 minutes.
2   Stir eggs, sifted dry ingredients and rum into the fruit mixture.
3   Grease 2-quart pudding steamer; spoon mixture into steamer. Top with pleated baking paper and foil; secure with kitchen string or lid.
4   Place pudding in 4½-quart slow cooker with enough boiling water to come halfway up side of steamer. Cook, covered, on high, 5 hours, replenishing with boiling water as necessary to maintain level.
5   Remove pudding from cooker, stand 10 minutes before turning onto plate.

prep + cook time 5 hours 30 minutes
nutritional count per serving
7.6g total fat (4.5g saturated fat); 350 cal; 61.5g carbohydrate; 4.1g protein; 3.7g fiber

tip The pleated paper and foil allow for the pudding mixture to rise.

❄ suitable to freeze at the end of step 5; pudding can be frozen as a whole pudding or in serving-sized wedges.

serving suggestion Serve with cream or custard.

creamy rice pudding with cinnamon sugar serves 6

1 cup uncooked white medium-grain rice
5 cups milk
½ cup superfine sugar
2-inch piece orange rind
1 vanilla bean
2 tablespoons superfine sugar, extra
1 teaspoon ground cinnamon

1 Combine rice, milk, sugar, and rind in 4½-quart slow cooker. Halve vanilla bean lengthwise; scrape seeds into cooker, add vanilla bean.
2 Cook, covered, on low, 6 hours, stirring twice, or until rice is tender. Discard vanilla bean and rind.

3 Combine extra sugar and cinnamon in small bowl, sprinkle over pudding.

prep + cook time 6 hours 10 minutes
nutritional count per serving
8.3g total fat (5.4g saturated fat); 362 cal; 61.5g carbohydrate; 9.3g protein; 0.3g fiber

tip The vanilla bean can be reused; wash and dry well, store in an airtight container or add to a container of sugar for vanilla-scented sugar.

❄ not suitable to freeze.

serving suggestion Serve warm pudding with canned, fresh, or stewed fruit drizzled with cream. (We stewed 5 ounces frozen raspberries with ¼ cup superfine sugar and 1 tablespoon of water.)

chocolate self-saucing pudding

serves 6

3 ounces butter
¾ cup milk
1 teaspoon vanilla extract
1 cup superfine sugar
1½ cups self-rising flour
2 tablespoons cocoa powder
1 egg, beaten lightly
1 cup firmly packed light brown sugar
2 tablespoons cocoa powder, extra
2½ cups boiling water

serving suggestion Serve pudding, hot or warm, dusted with a little sifted powdered sugar, and with cream and/or ice cream.

1 Grease 4½-quart slow cooker bowl.
2 Melt butter in milk over low heat in medium saucepan. Remove from heat; cool 5 minutes. Stir in extract and sugar, then sifted flour and cocoa, and egg. Spread mixture into cooker bowl.
3 Sift brown sugar and extra cocoa evenly over mixture; gently pour boiling water evenly over mixture. Cook, covered, on high, about 2½ hours or until center is firm.
4 Remove bowl from cooker. Stand pudding 5 minutes before serving.

prep + cook time 2 hours 50 minutes
nutritional count per serving
15.5g total fat (9.6g saturated fat); 580 cal; 101.3g carbohydrate; 6.9g protein; 1.6g fiber

❄ not suitable to freeze.

mandarin and almond pudding

serves 8

4 small mandarin oranges
4 eggs
⅔ cup superfine sugar
1⅓ cups ground almonds
⅔ cup self-rising flour

1 Place washed unpeeled mandarins in 4½-quart slow cooker; cover with hot water. Cook, covered, on high, 2 hours.
2 Trim ends from mandarins; discard. Halve mandarins; remove and discard seeds. Process mandarins, including rind, until mixture is pulpy.
3 Grease 2-quart pudding steamer.
4 Beat eggs and sugar in small bowl with electric mixer until thick and creamy; fold in ground almonds, sifted flour, and mandarin pulp. Spoon mixture into steamer. Top with pleated baking paper and foil; secure with kitchen string or lid.
5 Place pudding in cooker with enough boiling water to come halfway up side of steamer. Cook, covered, on high, 3 hours, replenishing with boiling water as necessary to maintain level. Stand pudding 5 minutes before turning onto plate.

prep + cook time 5 hours 30 minutes
nutritional count per serving
13.9g total fat (1.6g saturated fat); 298 cal; 32.5g carbohydrate; 9g protein; 3.2g fiber

tip The pleated paper and foil simply allow space for the pudding mixture to rise.

❄ not suitable to freeze.

serving suggestion Serve with cream, custard, or ice cream.

Glossary

ALLSPICE also known as pimento or Jamaican pepper; available whole or ground. Tastes like a blend of cinnamon, clove, and nutmeg—all spices.

ALMONDS, GROUND also known as almond meal; nuts are powdered to a coarse flour-like texture.

BACON SLICES made from cured, smoked pork.

BAKING SODA also known as bicarbonate of soda; a leavening agent.

BEANS
black turtle also known as black or black kidney beans; an earthy-flavored dried bean completely different from the better-known Chinese black beans (which are fermented soy beans).
cannellini small white bean that is similar in appearance and flavor to haricot, great northern, and navy beans, all of which can be substituted for the other.
green also known as French or string beans, this long thin fresh bean is consumed in its entirety once cooked.
kidney medium-sized red bean, slightly floury in texture yet sweet in flavor.
snake long (about 15 inches), thin, round, fresh green beans; Asian in origin, with a taste similar to green or French beans. They are also known as yard-long beans because of their length.

BEEF
brisket a cheaper cut from the belly; can be bought with or without bones as a joint for slow-roasting, or for stewing and casseroling as cubes or ground.
blade taken from the shoulder; this isn't as tender as other cuts of beef, it needs slow-roasting to achieve best results.
cheeks the cheek muscle of a cow. It's a very tough and lean cut of meat and is most often used for braising or slow cooking to produce a tender result.
chuck from the neck and shoulder of the beef; tends to be chewy but flavorful and inexpensive. A good cut for stewing or braising.
corned brined top round also known as topside roast; sold vacuum-sealed in brine.
osso buco literally meaning "bone with a hole", osso buco is cut from the shin of the hind leg. It is also known as knuckle.
sausages seasoned and spiced minced beef mixed with cereal and packed into casings. Also known as snags or bangers.
shank, see shin (below).
shin also known as gravy beef or shank, cut from the lower shin of a cow.
short ribs cut from the rib section; they are usually larger, more tender and meatier than pork spare ribs.

BEETS also known as beetroot; firm, round root vegetable.

BOK CHOY also known as buk choy, pak choi, Chinese white cabbage, or Chinese chard; has a fresh, mild mustard taste.

BREADCRUMBS, STALE one- or two-day-old bread made into crumbs by grating, blending, or processing.

BUTTER use salted or unsalted (sweet) butter; 4 ounces equals one stick.

CAPERS, BABY those picked early are very small, fuller-flavored and more expensive than the full-size ones. Capers must be rinsed well before using.

CARAWAY a member of the parsley family; available in seed or ground form. Has a pungent aroma and a distinctly sweet, but tangy, flavor.

CARDAMOM can be purchased in pod, seed, or ground form. Has a distinctive aromatic, sweetly rich flavor.

CARROTS, BABY small, sweet, and sold in bunches with the tops still attached.

CAVOLO NERO, or Tuscan cabbage, is a staple in Tuscan country cooking. It has long, narrow, wrinkled leaves and a rich and astringent, mild cabbage flavor. It doesn't lose its volume like chard or spinach when cooked, but it does need longer cooking.

CHICKEN
drumsticks leg with skin and bone intact.

thigh cutlets thigh with skin and center bone intact; sometimes found skinned with bone intact.

thigh filets thigh with skin and center bone removed.

CHILI available in many types and sizes. Use rubber gloves when seeding and chopping fresh chilies as they can burn your skin. Removing membranes and seeds lessens the heat level.

cayenne pepper dried, long, thin-fleshed, extremely hot ground red chili.

flakes dried, deep-red, dehydrated chili slices and whole seeds.

long green any unripened chili.

long red available both fresh and dried; a generic term used for any moderately hot, long (2in-3in), thin chili.

powder can be used as a substitute for fresh chilies (½ teaspoon ground chili powder to 1 medium chopped fresh chili).

CHINESE COOKING WINE also known as hao hsing or Chinese rice wine; made from fermented rice, wheat, sugar, and salt with a 13.5 percent alcohol content. Found in Asian food shops; if you can't find it, replace with mirin or sherry.

COCOA POWDER also known as cocoa; dried, unsweetened, roasted then ground cocoa beans (cacao seeds).

CORIANDER the leaves, stems and roots of coriander are used in Thai cooking; wash roots well before using. Also available ground or as seeds; do not substitute these for fresh coriander as the tastes are completely different.

CRANBERRIES, DRIED have the same slightly sour, succulent flavor as fresh cranberries. Available in supermarkets.

CREAM we use fresh cream, also known as heavy cream and light cream, unless otherwise stated.

CUMIN also known as zeera or comino; has a spicy, nutty flavor, and is available in seed form or dried and ground.

CURRY LEAVES available fresh or dried and have a mild curry flavor; use like bay leaves.

CURRY PASTES some recipes in this book call for commercially prepared pastes of varying strengths and flavors. Use whichever one you feel best suits your spice-level tolerance.

korma paste a mix of mostly heat-free spices, forms the base of a mild, almost nutty, slow-cooked curry.

powder a blend of ground spices that include chili, cinnamon, coriander, mace, fennel, fenugreek, cumin, cardamom, and turmeric. Can be mild or hot.

red probably the most popular curry paste; a hot blend of red chili, garlic, shallot, lemon grass, salt, galangal, shrimp paste, kaffir lime peel, coriander, cumin, and paprika. It is milder than the hotter Thai green curry paste.

rogan josh paste a medium-hot blend that is a specialty of Kashmir in northern India. It features tomatoes, fenugreek, coriander, paprika, and cumin.

EGGPLANT also known as aubergine.

baby also known as finger or Japanese eggplant; very small and slender so can be used without disgorging.

FENUGREEK a member of the pea family, the seeds have a bitter taste; the ground seeds are a traditional ingredient in Indian curries, powders, and pastes.

FIVE-SPICE POWDER (Chinese five-spice) a fragrant mixture of ground cinnamon, cloves, star anise, Sichuan pepper, and fennel seeds.

FLOUR

corn starch also known as cornflour; used as a thickening agent.

plain all-purpose flour made from wheat.

self-rising plain flour sifted with baking powder in the proportion of 1 cup flour to 2 teaspoons baking powder.

GARAM MASALA a blend of spices including cardamom, cinnamon, cloves, coriander, fennel, and cumin, roasted and ground together. Black pepper and chili can be added for a hotter version.

GHEE a type of clarified butter in which the milk solids are cooked until they are a golden brown, which imparts a nutty flavor and sweet aroma; this fat can be heated to a high temperature without burning. Available in the refrigerated section of supermarkets.

GINGER also known as green or root ginger; the thick root of a tropical plant.

ground also known as powdered ginger; used as a flavoring in cakes and pies but cannot be substituted for fresh ginger.

HARISSA a Moroccan sauce or paste made from dried chilies, cumin, garlic, oil, and caraway seeds; used as a rub for meats, a sauce, and dressing ingredient, or as a condiment eaten on its own. It is available from Middle-Eastern food shops and supermarkets.

HONEYCOMB TRIPE check with the butcher to make sure the tripe has been cleaned and blanched. We suggest you blanch the tripe again before cutting it into pieces. You might have to order the tripe from the butcher in advance.

HORSERADISH CREAM a paste of grated horseradish, mustard seeds, oil, and sugar.

LAMB
forequarter chops from the shoulder end of the sheep.
shanks, French-trimmed also known as drumsticks or Frenched shanks; the gristle and narrow end of the bone is discarded then the remaining meat trimmed.
shoulder boned from the shoulder. Very hard to carve with the bone in; to make carving easier, butchers will bone it and sell it as a boneless rolled shoulder.

LEEK a member of the onion family; looks like a giant green onion but is more subtle and mild in flavor.
baby, or pencil leeks, essentially young, slender leeks available early in the season, can be cooked and eaten like asparagus.

LENTILS (red, brown, yellow) dried pulses identified by and named after their color.

MARSALA a sweet, fortified wine to which additional alcohol has been added, most commonly in the form of brandy. It is available in a range of styles, from sweet to dry.

MIXED DRIED FRUIT a mix of raisins, currants, mixed citrus peel, and cherries.

MOROCCAN SEASONING available from most Middle-Eastern food stores, spice shops and major super-markets. Turmeric, cinnamon, and cumin add authentic Moroccan flavoring to dishes.

MUSHROOMS
button small, cultivated white mushrooms with a mild flavor.
portobello mature cremini. Large, dark brown mushrooms with full-bodied flavor; ideal for filling or barbecuing.

MUSSELS must be tightly closed when bought, indicating they are alive. Before cooking, scrub the shells with a strong brush and remove the "beards". Discard shells that do not open during cooking.

MUSTARD
dijon pale brown, distinctively flavored, fairly mild-tasting french mustard.
seeds, black also known as brown mustard seeds; more pungent than the yellow (or white) seeds used in prepared mustards.
whole grain also known as seeded. A French-style coarse-grain mustard made from crushed mustard seeds and dijon-style French mustard.

OILS
olive made from ripened olives. Extra virgin and virgin are the best, while extra light or light refers to taste, not fat levels.
peanut pressed from ground peanuts; most commonly used oil in Asian cooking because of its high smoke point (capacity to handle high heat without burning).
sesame made from roasted, crushed, white sesame seeds; a flavoring rather than a cooking medium.
vegetable oils sourced from plants rather than animal fats.

OLIVES
black have a richer and more mellow flavor than the green ones and are softer in texture. Sold either plain or in a piquant marinade.
green those harvested before fully ripened and are, as a rule, denser and more bitter than their black relatives.

ONIONS
baby also known as pickling onions and cocktail onions; are baby brown onions, though are larger than shallots.
brown and white are interchangeable, however, white onions have a more pungent flesh.
red also known as Spanish, red Spanish, or Bermuda onion; a sweet-flavored, large, purple-red onion.

PAPRIKA ground, dried, sweet red bell pepper; there are many types available, including sweet, hot, mild, and smoked.

PATTY-PAN SQUASH also known as crookneck or custard marrow pumpkins; a round, slightly flat summer squash that's yellow to pale-green in color, with a scalloped edge. It has a firm white flesh and a distinct flavor.

PEPPERCORNS, BLACK picked when the berry is not quite ripe, then dried until it shrivels and the skin turns dark brown/black. It's the strongest flavored of the three (white, green, and black)—slightly hot with a hint of sweetness.

PIE SPICE a blend of ground spices usually consisting of cinnamon, allspice, and nutmeg.

PISTACHIOS delicately flavored green nuts inside hard off-white shells. Available salted or unsalted. We always use shelled nuts in our recipes.

POLENTA also known as cornmeal; a flour-like cereal made of dried corn (maize) sold ground in several different textures; also the name of the dish made from it.

PORK
ham hock the lower portion of the leg; includes the meat, fat, and bone. Most have been cured, smoked or both, but fresh hocks are sometimes available.
neck sometimes called pork scotch; a boneless cut from the foreloin.
pickled pork brined legs or hocks. You may need to order this from the butcher in advance.
shoulder sold with bone in or out.

spare ribs well-trimmed mid-loin ribs.

POTATOES, BABY NEW not a separate variety but an early harvest with very thin skin; good unpeeled, steamed, and eaten, hot or cold, in salads.

POWDERED GRAVY MIX an instant gravy mix made with browned flour. All-purpose flour can be used instead for thickening. Available from supermarkets in a variety of flavors.

PRAWNS also known as shrimp.

PRESERVED LEMON RIND a North African specialty; lemons are quartered and preserved in salt and lemon juice or water. To use, remove and discard pulp, squeeze juice from rind, rinse rind well; slice thinly. Sold in delicatessens and major supermarkets.

RAISINS dried sweet grapes.

RAS EL HANOUT a classic spice blend used in Moroccan cooking. The name means "top of the shop" and is the very best spice blend a spice merchant has to offer. Most versions contain over a dozen spices, including cardamom, mace, nutmeg, cinnamon, and ground chili.

RICE
basmati a white, fragrant long-grained rice. Wash several times before cooking. medium-grain previously sold as calrose rice; extremely versatile rice that can be

substituted for short- or long-grain rices if necessary.

RISONI small, rice-shaped pasta similar to orzo; used in soups and salads.

ROMANO CHEESE a hard, sheep's- or cow's-milk cheese. Straw-colored and grainy in texture, it's mainly used for grating. Parmesan can be substituted.

SAFFRON available in strands (threads) or ground form; imparts a yellow-orange color to food once infused. Quality varies greatly; the best is the most expensive spice in the world. Should be stored in the freezer.

SAUCES
char siu a Chinese barbecue sauce made from sugar, water, salt, fermented soy bean paste, honey, soy sauce, malt syrup, and spices. Found at most supermarkets.
fish also called nam pla or nuoc nam; made from pulverized salted fermented fish, most often anchovies. Has a very pungent smell and strong taste, so use according to your taste level.
oyster Asian in origin, this rich, brown sauce is made from oysters and their brine, cooked with salt and soy sauce, and thickened with starches.
soy also known as sieu, is made from fermented soy beans. Several variations are available in most supermarkets and Asian food stores. We use a mild Japanese variety in our recipes; possibly the best table soy and the one to choose if you only want one variety.
light soy a fairly thin, pale but salty tasting sauce; used in dishes in which the natural color of the ingredients is to

be maintained. Not to be confused with salt-reduced or low-sodium soy sauces.
tamari a thick, dark soy sauce made mainly from soy beans without the wheat used in standard soy sauces.
tomato pasta made from a blend of tomatoes, herbs, and spices.
Worcestershire a dark-colored condiment made from garlic, soy sauce, tamarind, onions, molasses, lime, anchovies, vinegar, and seasonings.

SAUSAGES ground meat seasoned with salt and spices, mixed with cereal and packed into casings. Also known as bangers.
italian pork a pork sausage often added to pasta sauces. Varieties include sweet Italian sausage, which is flavored with garlic and fennel seed, and hot Italian sausage, which has chili.

SOUR CREAM a thick commercially-cultured soured cream. Minimum fat content 35 percent.

SOURDOUGH has a lightly sour taste from the yeast starter culture used to make the bread. A low-risen bread with a dense center and crisp crust.

SUGAR
dark brown a moist, dark brown sugar with a rich distinctive full flavor coming from natural molasses syrup.
light brown a soft, finely granulated sugar retaining molasses for its characteristic color and flavor.
superfine also known as caster or finely granulated table sugar.

white a coarsely granulated table sugar, also known as crystal sugar.

TAMARI see sauces.

TAMARIND CONCENTRATE the distillation of tamarind pulp into a condensed, compacted paste with a sweet-sour, slightly astringent taste. Thick and purple-black, it requires no soaking or straining. Found in Asian food stores and supermarkets.

TOFU also known as bean curd, an off-white, custard-like product made from the "milk" of crushed soy beans; comes fresh as soft or firm. Leftover fresh tofu can be refrigerated in water (which is changed daily) for up to 4 days.
silken tofu refers to the method by which it is made—where it is strained through silk.

TOMATOES
paste triple-concentrated tomato puree.
puree canned pureed tomatoes (not tomato paste). Substitute with fresh peeled and pureed tomatoes.
roma also called plum; these are smallish, oval-shaped tomatoes commonly used in Italian cooking or salads.

TORTILLAS thin, round unleavened bread originating in Mexico. Two kinds are available, one made from wheat flour and the other from corn.

TURMERIC, GROUND a member of the ginger family, its root is dried and ground, resulting in the rich yellow powder that gives many

Indian dishes their characteristic yellow color. It is intensely pungent in taste but not hot.

VANILLA EXTRACT made by extracting the flavor from the vanilla bean pod; the pods are soaked, usually in alcohol, to capture the authentic flavor.

VINEGAR
balsamic made from the juice of Trebbiano grapes; it is a deep rich brown color with a sweet and sour flavor.
white balsamic is a clear and lighter version of balsamic vinegar; it has a fresh, sweet, clean taste.
brown malt made from fermented malt and beech shavings.
cider (apple cider) made from fermented apples.
white made from the spirit of cane sugar.
white wine made from a blend of white wines.

WALNUTS a rich, flavorful nut. Should be plump and firm, not shriveled or soft. Has a high oil content so store in the refrigerator. Pecans can be substituted.

WHITE SWEET POTATO is less sweet than orange sweet potato; has an earthy flavor. It has a purple flesh beneath its white skin.

YOGURT we use plain yogurt unless otherwise indicated.

ZUCCHINI small green, yellow, or white vegetable belonging to the squash family.

Index

Conversion Chart

MEASURES

All cup and spoon measurements are level. The most accurate way to measure dry ingredients is to use a spoon to fill the measuring cup, without packing or scooping with the cup, and leveling off the top with a straight edge.

When measuring liquids, use a clear glass or plastic liquid measuring cup with markings on the side.

As a general rule for casserole, stew, curry, and tagine recipes in a slow cooker, the cooker insert should always be at least half full. Place the vegetables into the cooker, put the meat on top of the vegetables, then add the liquid. When preparing soup in a slow cooker, the ingredients should also fill the cooking chamber at least half full.

DRY MEASURES

METRIC	IMPERIAL
15g	½oz
30g	1oz
60g	2oz
90g	3oz
125g	4oz (¼lb)
155g	5oz
185g	6oz
220g	7oz
250g	8oz (½lb)
280g	9oz
315g	10oz
345g	11oz
375g	12oz (¾lb)
410g	13oz
440g	14oz
470g	15oz
500g	16oz (1lb)
750g	24oz (1½lb)
1kg	32oz (2lb)

LIQUID MEASURES

METRIC	IMPERIAL
30ml	1 fluid oz
60ml	2 fluid oz
100ml	3 fluid oz
125ml	4 fluid oz
150ml	5 fluid oz (¼ pint/1 gill)
190ml	6 fluid oz
250ml	8 fluid oz
300ml	10 fluid oz (½ pint)
500ml	16 fluid oz
600ml	20 fluid oz (1 pint)
1000ml (1 liter)	1¾ pints

LENGTH MEASURES

3mm	⅛in
6mm	¼in
1cm	½in
2cm	¾in
2.5cm	1in
5cm	2in
6cm	2½in
8cm	3in
10cm	4in
13cm	5in
15cm	6in
18cm	7in
20cm	8in
23cm	9in
25cm	10in
28cm	11in
30cm	12in (1ft)

OVEN TEMPERATURES

These oven temperatures are only a guide for conventional ovens. For fan-forced ovens, check the manufacturer's manual.

	°F (FAHRENHEIT)	°C (CELSIUS)
Very slow	250	120
Slow	275–300	150
Moderately slow	325	160
Moderate	350–375	180
Moderately hot	400	200
Hot	425-450	220
Very hot	475	240

DELISH
Elizabeth Shepard   Executive Director

Content contained in this book was originally published by ACP Magazines Limited and is reproduced with permission.

Photography by Ian Wallace
U.S. Edition packaged by LightSpeed Publishing, Inc.; design by X-Height Studio; Culinary Americanization: Wes Martin

Library of Congress Cataloging-in-Publication Data Available

10 9 8 7 6 5 4 3 2 1

Published by Hearst Books
A division of Sterling Publishing Co., Inc.
387 Park Avenue South, New York, NY 10016

Delish is a registered trademark of Hearst Communications, Inc.

www.delish.com

For information about custom editions, special sales, premium and corporate purchases, please contact Sterling Special Sales Department at 800-805-5489 or specialsales@sterlingpublishing.com.

Distributed in Canada by Sterling Publishing
c/o Canadian Manda Group, 165 Dufferin Street
Toronto, Ontario, Canada M6K 3H6

Manufactured in China

Sterling ISBN 978-1-58816-933-4